After all that Larry—and by extension Sharon—has done for me and my family over the last twenty years, I have deep appreciation for him. From the golf outings to Rent One Day at Rent One Park to all the Cardinals baseball games, not to mention the amazing Mexico trips that we all love. We know you do it all because you care and because you want to, not because you have to. Thank you. I look forward to many more years under your direction continuing to grow my store.

—JOE TUBB

Store manager, Poplar Bluff

Larry and Sharon have provided me a place to succeed. They are truly people who care for their business and employees. When my daughter was going through surgery for her back, they went out of their way to have a fundraiser. They even offered to open their home to me while she was in the hospital. When I do interviews for potential new hires, I always share this story of how you care. Thank you for entrusting me to manage your Anna location. Thank you for having 401(k)s for your employees to look toward their future. Thank you for the company retreats; I know you invest a lot of time and money to do this for your employees. I can never say enough that it is my honor and privilege to work for you and this great company.

—WADE MARKS

Store manager, Anna, Illinois

Own Your
Life

ON BUILDING A
FAMILY BUSINESS AND
LEAVING A LEGACY

Own Your Life

SHARON & LARRY CARRICO

Published by Advantage Books, Charleston, South Carolina.
An imprint of Advantage Media.

ADVANTAGE is a registered trademark, and the Advantage colophon is a trademark of Advantage Media Group, Inc.

Printed in the United States of America.

10 9 8 7 6 5 4 3 2 1

ISBN: 978-1-64225-827-1 (Paperback)
ISBN: 978-1-64225-826-4 (eBook)

Library of Congress Control Number: 2023908431

Cover design by Megan Elger.

This publication is designed to provide accurate and authoritative information in regard to the subject matter covered. It is sold with the understanding that the publisher is not engaged in rendering legal, accounting, or other professional services. If legal advice or other expert assistance is required, the services of a competent professional person should be sought.

Advantage Books is an imprint of Advantage Media Group. Advantage Media helps busy entrepreneurs, CEOs, and leaders write and publish a book to grow their business and become the authority in their field. Advantage authors comprise an exclusive community of industry professionals, idea-makers, and thought leaders. For more information go to **advantagemedia.com**.

Our legacy is our family, coworkers, and close friends.
We lived the American dream.

CONTENTS

ACKNOWLEDGMENTS

Special thanks to our parents, who with so little gave so much to ensure us a strong education and faith foundation and who loved and supported us unconditionally at every step of our journey. We also appreciate that our success is the result of so many coworkers, friends, and partners along the way. We cannot mention them all, but if you were part of any of our many companies, jobs, or dreams, we appreciate the work you put in, the significance you played, and the difference you made. We are especially grateful for all those who helped us raise our own children, friends, family, and everyone in between. From daycare to college, from game days to wedding days, you made an impact when you touched their lives with care and goodness. Thank you.

INTRODUCTION

W hen we got married in 1983, all we knew was that we wanted more than what we had and that together was the surest way to get it. So we got married, purchased our first company, and began working for our dream, one that was about more than just success.

By 1999, just over a decade later, we had moved nine times, nearly lost the business for incorrect tax collection, survived a fire that razed our main store/corporate office (and an entire city block), rescued a failing marriage by facing addiction head-on, and were struggling to raise our three kids to live out their best potential. That we made it and succeeded to have the life we have now took a lot of days just doing the next right thing, never giving up on each other, and having a constant faith that God held it all.

This book tells our story in the hope it encourages you to live yours. We began with nothing and are now blessed with so much. If you think success is not meant for you or that the American dream can't happen in today's political and economic climate, this book is for you. In these pages you will witness how that dream begins in lessons taught by parents, what the dream is for us, how it constantly changes, and some of the things that can get in your way or make it feel impossible.

We barely had a plan at first. We just showed up and showed up and showed up and learned along the way. From rent-to-own to marketing, from internet service providers to homeland security, from real estate to service and repair, we just kept showing up. We looked to others for guidance, education, motivation, and inspiration. Today, we are blessed to find success in business, in love, and in life. We are excited to share some of what we learned along the way with you.

In this book we talk about what worked and what didn't, and we take a peek at how all these ventures impacted our lives at home. The joy of being business owners, community supporters, parents, and grandparents is all the sweeter because the road was not always clear or smooth (and you're going to read about a lot of those bumps in the road!). It is our genuine hope that our mistakes, missteps, and life lessons will inspire you with the grace of faith, forgiveness, and fortitude we rely on every day. No matter what shadows of doubt and despair we face, they will eventually fade in the light of love. We hope you see, as we do, that life is beautiful, always.

And so we begin where it begins for all of us, the most fun part of our story: our growing-up years. We hope you enjoy the tale!

CHAPTER ONE

The Paperboy and the Schoolgirl

> There are no perfect parents, and there are
> no perfect children, but there are plenty
> of perfect moments along the way.
>
> —DAVE WILLIS

Sharon: Life Taking Shape

Human nature compels us to believe we are self-made, that we can shape our lives and master our own destiny. In reality we are all the products of those who came before us and before them and before them. Our lives are built on foundations laid by people we never met whose lives ended before ours began. However, those foundations inform our origin, not our destiny. The foundation is simply the stability of our launch point.

My launch point was nestled in an average American foundation. My parents ascended from barely middle class to solidly middle class during my elementary school years. Their long and loving marriage was inspiring but, like any marriage, not without its challenges. Over their sixty-seven years together, they endured their share of struggles and even a separation, but they chose to stick it out, and, with time and more than a little prayer, it got better and better.

My earliest memories of them together, when I was very young, include a fair share of yelling, tears, and fears. With never enough money, never enough time, it seemed there was never enough of anything but frustration and anger. I can still hear dishes breaking, furniture crashing, and doors slamming from behind my childhood bedroom door. Yet, I also remember errands in the car and my mom belting out "Ave Maria" with absolute abandon. My fondest memories include being "dropped" into bed, then tucked in so tight by my dad that I could barely wiggle. His warmth and affection sent me off to sleep in a cocoon of security. As a little girl, I nearly wore out his feet, dancing on them in the living room. I only learned late in life that good times and bad times almost always coexist for all of us, all the time. But when I was young, I thought it was just one or the other, good or bad, happy or sad, rich or poor, and thus assumed my parents as a couple were certainly doomed.

Yet, by the time I graduated from college, they were traveling together across America in the pickup truck my dad converted to a camper. Mom's eyes twinkled as she told me she might need one of those signs to put out at the campsite that said, "If this camper is rockin', don't come knockin'." I can't tell you how that transition happened—if it started during my self-obsessed high school years or in their empty nest while I was away at college. Regardless of when it happened, all I know is that they stuck it out and, thankfully, reaped the well-earned rewards together for many years.

Though they bickered nearly nonstop some days and drove each other crazy on others, they ended up best friends and true loves. Their example of love and determination forms the foundations I've brought to my own marriage, my motherhood, and my work. My parents' model of persistence as a couple was honest, encouraging, and comforting. It gave me strength. It still gives me strength. I treasure a picture of them I captured in 2017, after sixty-four years of marriage, as they walked hand in hand into the hospital for Dad's MRI to confirm his Alzheimer's diagnosis. He was eighty-two, she was eighty-three, and they were inseparable by then, having left their anger, fear, and regret in a shared but distant past.

Although the Bible tells us, "The two shall become one," we should not take that too literally or as an incantation that magically makes it true. Every marriage involves a tinge of power struggle, a bit of identity crisis, varying degrees of codependency, and a lot of autonomy. After nearly two years of dating, when they married, my dad was just eighteen, and Mom all of nineteen—they were babies!—but babies who, like most teenagers, had already lived a lifetime as individuals before confidently strutting together into whatever was next.

My mom knew difficult times much too early in life. She lost her mother when she was just nine years old. The youngest of five children, she was raised by an adoring father and, admittedly, spoiled by him. She lived with him all her life, and even after marrying, the newlyweds shared his home. They moved out after my brother was born, and my mom's father died shortly after, when she was in her early twenties, before I was born. Her dad was her hero, and she still regrets moving out, feeling guilty for not being there when he died, even at eighty-eight. Her oldest sister by ten years, Florence, was like a second mother, and my mom would seek her for comfort and advice all of her life.

Many families might lose touch without a matriarch or patriarch to gather them up, or maybe they just grow apart and hold reunions once in a while. However, my mom and her siblings were tight all the way through; they remained so close that, come hell or high water, they vacationed together just the five of them every summer for nearly ten years, even after we kids were grown. Most often they went to Florida and stayed with Jim, the only brother. They had adventures to Disney World, the Everglades, seafood festivals, Sanibel Island, and lots of days lazing by his pool. The stories they could tell would fill a book.

Those aunts, uncles, and cousins were the best family. Countless fish fries, turtle mulligans, late-night poker games, and kid swaps created a lifetime of memories. Florence lived in Long Beach, Mississippi, so each summer we spent a week there, learning how to crab, evading jelly fish, building drip-drop sandcastles, exploring sandbars, blistering and peeling, and growing up in all the best ways. They lived just two blocks from the beach, and on the walks home, we would sneak into the Holiday Inn swimming pool to rinse off the salt and sand. In the evenings after dinner, my cousins and I were allowed to go to the snow cone shack a few blocks down the road and treat ourselves, by ourselves. All these years later, I'm not sure which was better—those dusky walks under mossy oaks or that icy-sweet coconut-banana combination. It's probably the combined power of hot nights, cold treats, and bold independence that keeps this beloved memory so fresh.

My uncle lived just a few miles from our house in a small, rural village called Shiloh, Illinois. He had a huge garden and acres of grounds, and he even kept a pony and chickens for a while. His five boys would greet us, and we'd trek the nearby woods, parks, and fields with abandon. We made explorations in the creek bed, expeditions down the gully, treasure hunts at the dump, and competitions at the mulberry tree, and we never knew a moment of boredom. My aunt couldn't keep up with all their antics or their mess. The house always seemed in shambles; they even had a guinea pig living in a corner of the kitchen at one point—no cage, just a bit of chicken wire fencing off the corner where he happily waited for someone to give him attention and kitchen scraps.

At my home things were more sedate. I was expected to put everything back where it belonged, take off my shoes, and wipe the bathroom sink after I washed my hands. I knew the rigid protocols of my own home were extreme, but my cousins' chaos was the opposite extreme. I always did a few dishes when we visited. I carried whatever mess I could up the back stairs to help and be a gracious guest. But, no matter how I tried to help, you really couldn't tell any difference. I loved it there anyway.

My favorite aunt lived directly across the street from us. It seemed we shared everything between our houses—sugar and toilet paper, meals and errands and secrets. One summer my dad set up an above-ground pool in our backyard, but it was taking too long to fill from our single outdoor tap. To speed the process, we went around the neighborhood borrowing hoses and ran them from my aunt's house across the street to the pool in our backyard. I guess we even shared the water bill.

In all I was blessed with seventeen cousins, and thanks to them I grew up never knowing there were other ways to be a family. To me family was everyone and everything, together. The best part of every family gathering, no doubt, was the freedom my mom's trust and comfort in her brother and sisters and their children provided me.

Maybe growing up during the Depression when there was never enough made her hold on too tightly. Maybe because she lost her parents so young, she clung to her children with ferocity. Maybe her generation, when everyone aspired to be June Cleaver, made her feel a sense of lacking or inadequacy. Whatever drove her or haunted her eventually manifested in obsessive-compulsive disorder and overprotectiveness. She watched me like a hawk, and we cleaned that house like our lives depended on it. My time with aunts, uncles, and cousins brought freedom and balance in comparison to her ever-watchful eye and high expectations at home. Extended family can give us so much and teaches us so much more about ourselves and the world around us than parents alone can do.

In addition to her strong family bonds, my mom's faith got her through the difficulties of losing her parents and the struggles of being a young wife and mother in the 1960s. She went to an all-girls Catholic high school and was taught that faith meant adherence to the rules, and the rules were set by the Church. My dad converted to please her; he was just eighteen, and it was a condition to marrying her that was not debatable. I don't remember him attending church when I was young, unless it was for a ceremony like a baptism, confirmation, funeral, or wedding. As much as Mom was about following the rules and the Church, Dad was not. He was a free spirit in his youth, a high school dropout with a tattoo and a motorcycle, sporting a greaser hairstyle that he wore better than Elvis from the pics I've seen.

Mom was different. Catholicism was Mom's guiding star in the earliest years of my own childhood. The consistency and security of faith and Catholic ritual helped keep her fears in check. In turn Mom was the guiding star in our family, and there was no way her children would not be raised Catholic! As soon as the time came, she sent me and my big brother, Denny, to St. Henry's Catholic Grade School, where I thrived.

I adored everything about school and was good at it. My success at school, however, was academic only. When I look at those glowing report cards, there are more than a few marks next to "improve self-control." All I know is those nuns had high standards, and everyone always said I was my father's daughter. I remember trying so hard to be attentive and accommodating; I was always polite and helpful, but sitting still was just not in my DNA.

School was a safe and socially acceptable place to explore the emerging world of the late 1960s, but the world would not be kept at bay. By the time I reached middle school in the early '70s, the civil rights movement, desegregation, Vietnam, and ultimately the women's movement all influenced the way my brother, my friends, and I saw the world around us. Things were changing, and we were changing. Though our daily lives seemed simple, and while we were entertained nightly by *Laugh-In*, Red Skelton, or Dean Martin, the adult conversations and fears were constantly playing in the background. I had cousins in Vietnam, a brother with a draft card, a "hippie" cousin in jail in Mississippi, and a mom who had moved from being a secretary to a civil service G5 position at the local air force base—and we walked on the moon—all in a single decade. Few times in history are as chaotic as the period when I grew up, and watching my parents brace themselves and, at times, chafe at these changes taught me early to keep my mind open and my curiosity sharp.

Larry: The Paperboy

Dad and Mom both worked hard. Dad worked at the General Motors plant in St. Louis and was a proud union man. He never worked an unpaid hour, because that would have gone against his belief that if you showed up for work, you got paid for your time. He had a sixth-grade education, but Dad got on at GM as a young man, and through his hard work he built a long career.

Dad put in long hours on the production line. When he got home exhausted from work around three thirty, he would lie on the couch and watch a bit of TV before dinner around four o'clock or so. He started work early and had his dinner early. After dinner he'd relax in his underwear for the evening with a beer in hand. He did enjoy his TV; we were one of the first with a twenty-five-inch TV, and because of the heat in the summer, we had a window air conditioner before most too. These were Dad's two luxury items he acquired with his hard-earned wages in our small home.

The house where I spent the majority of my childhood was at most eight hundred square feet with a basement, if you could call it that. Our living room shared one wall with my parents' bedroom and another wall with the kitchen. The four of us shared a tiny bathroom, and the small bedroom I shared with my little brother, Keith, was added when we were very young. Down in the basement was an old-fashioned wringer washer and rinse tub sharing limited space with the hulking old furnace. My playroom/clubhouse was a ten-by-ten space where we hosted our neighborhood club meetings—it had also held the coal bin in years past. I didn't know any different, and as far as I was concerned, life was good.

When money got tight, Mom waited tables and bartended. She would come home in her white waitress smock and the smoke and french-fry smells that clung to her always overwhelmed me in our tiny kitchen. Even so I would sit at the table and help her separate and count the coins she earned in East St. Louis. We were a working-class family in a working-class neighborhood. Work was not only a means to survive, but also the lifeblood of our community. My parents and their peers were old enough to remember times when there wasn't enough work to go around, so they embraced the work available to them.

When Mom and Dad weren't working for their pay, they were working for our community. During the time I played Khoury League baseball, Dad coached the team I was on with my brother, was on the board, and cut the grass at the playing field, and Mom managed the concession stand for the eight games that stretched on through each evening for almost eight years.

Mom would spend her spare time driving elderly neighbors to their appointments and baking for the neighbors. She was a giving woman who sought each opportunity to give back to the community.

Community was bolstered by family. Weekends included barbecues and horseshoe games, usually at my uncle Larry or aunt Louise's home. My uncle Tom and his five kids were in walking distance and hosted our daily play times. My kid brother, Keith, hung out with Mary, the youngest of the five, while I played with the three older boys, Tommy, Johnny, and Pat. I could easily walk to their house, and we walked together to the local Catholic school.

Mom had a big Southern Baptist family from Ravenden, Arkansas. They all came from a farm community and picked cotton as kids. Mom was bitten by a rattlesnake as a child and almost died from it. To treat it the men of the family came and cut away the bite and sucked the venom out, spitting it in the dirt next to the cotton rows. Mom was sent to the house for a day to get patched up and rest, and then she was back in the fields the next day. To this day I can close my eyes and see that scar on her leg the size of a fifty-cent piece—some scars leave deep marks in our memories.

Misadventure and loss marked Mom's side of the family. A baby boy was lost during the winter when the family hosted a large gathering, and after the first person tossed a coat over the baby on the bed, no one saw him, and the guests' coats kept piling up over the little guy, and he suffocated. Such a tragedy is remembered through the generations.

Life was rough for Mom and her surviving seven brothers and sisters, especially my beloved aunt Gracie. Gracie left Arkansas for East St. Louis in her teens. Gracie had two boys and four girls. Her younger son, Floyd, was a close friend to me and my cousin. Her older son, Roy, served in Vietnam, and Floyd was just a teenager when he was lost in a car accident. Like Uncle Bill, Larry, and Tom on Dad's side, Aunt Gracie on Mom's side was the core of the family gatherings. If we ever had a vacation, it was to visit family. We never ran low on family connections, and because we were so close, we felt losses like Floyd's deeply.

Even though she converted to marry Dad, Mom didn't go to Mass with us on Sundays. As I got older, I wondered why she didn't have to go if I did. She might not have been the most devout convert, but when opening the door from church on Sunday, we could always depend on Mom to have the salt-cured bacon cooking for breakfast when we got home. Her explanation was that church wasn't the difference maker, but your kindness and actions to others were. She lived that faith every day.

For me though, church was one of the many things that filled my days as a kid. I was there six days a week for at least eight years while in grade school and was blessed because I only had to walk one hundred yards to the entrance of the school and church. I went out our back door to school five days a week and the front door of our home on Sundays for church. Summer was always a relief, because there was no school or church through the weekdays.

Like Mom and Dad, I worked. When I was eleven years old, I started delivering my papers after school at three thirty. During the week delivering ninety-six papers was a breeze. Saturday's paper delivery, however, was larger than the whole week because of the paper's added bulk from advertisements and special weekly sections. I tried to franchise work to my cousins, but sometimes they didn't show up. Their absence wasn't as hard on me on weekdays, but when they skipped out on a Saturday evening paper, I had to drag a hundred pounds of paper through my neighborhood, making sure all my customers were satisfied. The work was hardest the first block, but the load lightened as I persisted. Occasionally, I would be asked to pick up additional routes because others failed to show; of course no one ever quit their route on Monday. They always waited until Saturday, and then I was back to the heavy loads, but it was all an important education.

I also had to balance the customer satisfaction with the bottom line, learning how to do collections before I learned algebra. I knew full well the value of customer service and showing up early by the age of twelve.

Even though I was busy with school and sports, I always sought more work. Over the summers I worked on a farm where we started at five in the morning on Saturdays, and sometimes fights were part of the entertainment. It was a rough time for boys, but I did what I had to do to fit in and not stand out. When I was fifteen, work found me beneath a highway in a dark hole attempting to feel my way to repair an irrigation line on the farm. My first attempt failed, and I was trapped in the dark with muskrats and muck until I got it right. When I finally fixed the line, all the sprinkler heads ran, and my work was done for the day. Doing that taught me I could do hard things, that I wasn't above doing my part, but it also taught me that I wanted to stay above ground. That work ethic and spirit of service came directly from Mom and Dad and their loyalty to family and community.

Sharon: Independence Blooming

I moved from St. Henry's to public school in seventh grade, where my love of learning temporarily took a back seat to middle school priorities: school dances, sleepovers, playground turf wars, first kisses, and Friday nights at the skating rink. By middle school my mom had soured on attending church every Sunday, and if she didn't go, I didn't go. For whatever reason her faith was taking a back seat for now. At home Mom and Dad had fights about money, and Denny's Catholic high school tuition came up a lot. Most of my neighborhood friends went to public school, so it wasn't even questioned the day I said, "I want to go to West Junior High next year."

Middle school can be killer for kids, and my mom hated all the drama that came with it. For me though, I remember it as a time when I had a posse of girlfriends and something going on all the time. We rode our bikes to the public pool almost every day in the summer and hung out on the street corner making daisy chains and talking about boys. In the extreme afternoon heat, we'd ride to the public library to linger in the cool aisles of books.

A favorite pastime was scavenging our houses for loose change and heading to the liquor store for a candy run or pooling our coins for a container of Cool Whip from the grocery store to split between us. Yes, we ate Cool Whip like it was ice cream. We knew every street and every shortcut in our town, and we relished our little world.

We spent most rainy or chilly days at Cheryl's or Pam's or Janelle's, playing endless games of Spades. We never went to Ellen's or Cindy's or Theresa's or my house. Funny how kids just know all the places where you can eat a container of Cool Whip in peace.

The summer after eighth grade, my dad built a family room onto our house and allowed me to be his assistant. I knew he was a whiz with motors and woodworking, and I'd spent many hours at his workbench in the garage or leaning over a car engine. I could run a table saw and a drill; I could change spark plugs in the lawnmower and check the oil on every car in the drive.

I knew my dad was handy from an early age. Yet, I had no idea he could actually build a room until we did it, together. From foundation to roof to electrical, he mapped it out and got it done. It's one of my favorite memories, and I can still see his prideful smile as I learned to hammer siding, install shingles, and clean up a job site. Always patient, ever understanding, he didn't push me to help but let me choose my path. One day I'd spend hours building with him, others I'd be off with my friends to the public pool or honing tennis skills on the back of the junior high. No matter where I went, he always welcomed me back with open arms and a warm smile.

As I entered high school, my brother, Denny, graduated and went on to junior college. Dad had finished the new addition and was working nights on the railroad. Mom worked full time, and her nights were spent catching up on the phone with family and friends, planning meals, or running errands. Money seemed to be a less volatile subject, and Mom and I had gotten in the habit of shopping downtown every Saturday.

She still weighed each purchase carefully—money was around but still tight—and we put everything on layaway. She always made sure I had what I needed: a new coat, new shoes, new jeans. I specifically remember planning to go to the sweetheart dance freshman year, shopping with her in all the stores, and putting *the* dress on layaway months ahead of time. We always had lunch before heading home, and she let me pick out songs on the jukebox at our favorite diner. I think I wore out "Delta Dawn" that year and still know every word.

Many of my middle school friends went to a different high school than me. The ones that did attend with me seemed to grow into themselves through extracurriculars like band, cheerleading, sports, or theater. I worked on the stage crew for a bit and joined the float committee for our class float in the homecoming parade. I hadn't really found my groove yet when a girl named Barb sat down next to me at the lunch table one day. She had the gift of gab (a very good kind of friend to have if you're an introvert like me) and seemed to know more than a little about everybody's business. I don't know exactly why, but we quickly became best friends, and to this day we still sign all of our cards "BFF." I hardly have a high school memory, outside the classroom, that doesn't include her. I never had a sister, and I always think it must be like having a Barb.

I spent many Saturday nights sleeping over at Barb's and attended her family's church with her on those Sunday mornings. She took me to her Lutheran youth group shortly after we met. I don't know what I was expecting, but it wasn't this awesome group of teens, who shared games, food, fun, and music, with a little Jesus mixed in.

The youth group practiced and performed a musical recital every year. Those songs and the fun we had at meetings and the traveling we did together to sing became my "extracurricular." It was where I fit in best during my early high school years.

What I'd learned as doctrine and followed out of obligation in grade school began to feel different in this new church. I got my first Bible and began reading it and asking questions. I have thanked Barb many times for initiating my true spiritual journey. I still get that Bible out from time to time to ponder my margin notes and highlights, reminding myself what a fourteen-year-old girl found of interest in there.

I turned fifteen January of my freshman year, and I got myself a work permit. My aunt was working as a waitress at a diner downtown, and they needed help. She said I'd be perfect and got me an interview. I had helped her out when I was ten or eleven, when she tried her luck as owner of a snack bar down the street from our house. I wasn't on payroll and didn't do a lot, but I loved the hustle of the place and seeing how much she loved it. I also shoveled snow and babysat and even mowed a few yards from time to time. But my first "real" job meant making real money (ninety-nine cents an hour plus tips) and saving for a car. Within a couple years, work would mean more than that, but at fifteen it was a taste of freedom to come; at age sixteen I would not only make my own money, but I could drive and date.

Turning sixteen was a game changer for me. I'd met a boy at the public pool the summer before, and even though I couldn't go on an official date until I was sixteen, he'd come by the house for visits or meet me out back where I worked. I'd ride my bike to the park and hop in his '57 Chevy, and we'd steal all the kisses and the secrets we could fit inside a twenty-minute whisp of time. He was my first real date, my first bottle of wine, my first and only sweetheart dance, and my first big breakup a couple months after that first date.

Barb and I dropped out of youth group at some point junior year. We were both working and running around with other friend groups. We were together so much that people called us Mutt and

Jeff in reference to a comic-strip friendship. We floated between social groups from the stadium club, where we went to smoke between classes, and the cheerleaders and jocks. We even had friend groups from the other two high schools in town, but we never really settled into any one place. I went to class, went to work, and drove Main Street on the weekends like everybody else. I had a couple boyfriends and some great memories, but for some reason, I don't know why, I just couldn't wait for it to be over so I could move on to my "real life."

Mom and I were butting heads more and more as I moved through high school. I never made curfew, she hated my boyfriends, or she loved the ones I didn't. I was drinking and staying out past curfew, and I had totaled my car. I threw a party when she and Dad went out of town one weekend. It got out of hand. Someone drove in the neighbor's yard and over a tree, and the road was blocked with cars, and the cops showed up. I was such a mess, hadn't planned on anything more than a few friends, and remember crawling on my hands and knees most of the night scouring the kitchen floor for beer caps and tabs so the newly installed linoleum wouldn't be cut when mom got back.

My brother retreated to my aunt's home across the street, and they just turned out the lights and went to bed. My aunt was not fazed by much, but my mom was enraged. The fight when she got home ended badly and brought out many things I'm not sure should have been said by either of us. Either way, she did not stop worrying, setting curfews, or calling friends to track me down until I went away to college.

Social life aside, my grades were always excellent, and my life *at* high school was much tamer. I took advanced classes and the hardest math and science classes the school offered. My brother, Denny, who had transferred to the University of Illinois after finishing junior college, noticed how easy it was for me to accomplish my grades. Though, like most older brothers, he had little interest in me as a younger sister, he did me an honor and a favor when he convinced our mom that I was too good to miss the chance to go to a proper university. He kept telling our mom that I needed to study engineering at the University of Illinois. Mom looked up to him, and he vouched for my potential. Ultimately, he convinced our mom to finally let me fly.

I found myself in Mr. Tollefson's office. He was our high school counselor, and I wanted help applying to the University of Illinois engineering department. He told me something I'll never forget: "You can apply, but you're not going to make it." Looking back it's a great example of the difference between a young man of Denny's generation and a middle-aged man of my parents' generation. The counselor didn't see my potential, but two of my favorite teachers (both women) were encouraging and wrote letters of recommendation. I applied to the University of Illinois and Illinois State University (my backup), and I was accepted to both.

The cost was, as cost always was, a concern. My mom and dad agreed to my proposal: they would pay the tuition if I paid for my books and incidentals. I'd been working for years by the time I graduated from high school and had saved money for college. Housing, however, was a challenge. Again, Denny came through and connected me to a sister of his friend. Through them we found a Baptist all-girl co-op house where I could sleep and eat for ninety-nine dollars a month. My future was just ahead, and I was ready!

Larry: Self-Made Man

Mom and Dad fought if they both drank. This was not a new thing, but it had grown old by the time I was sixteen when they finally decided to divorce. The agreement was amicable, and Mom moved close by. She stayed involved not just in our lives, but in Dad's extended family's lives. When she visited she still came to gatherings with the family on occasion and fit right in as if she'd never left.

Dad remarried quickly. He couldn't imagine being a single dad in the 1970s. I was almost grown, but Keith was only ten. I was busy with my own life, playing baseball, basketball, and soccer, going to school, and working at the farm or local liquor store after school. So, while I wouldn't say my parents' divorce didn't affect me, I was busy starting my own life and less interested in their lives, like any other high school kid.

The liquor store was a great after-school job. I made seventy-five cents an hour, which was significantly better than the mistakes I made attempting and failing at roofing and siding for the summer I was sixteen. Marvin and I didn't realize when bidding the jobs that we were supposed to remove the old roof shingles before laying down the new ones.

The liquor store was not in the hot sun on a roof, not in the dark rat-filled space beneath a highway, and though there were heavy boxes to move, it paid better than the paper routes. It also put me in exactly the right place at exactly the right time. One afternoon the PA system at Assumption High School in East St. Louis requested my presence at the counselor's office. My first thought was I was in trouble, but I couldn't imagine for what. I hadn't forged any teachers' signatures or left the campus in several weeks. It turned out to be good news. A new mall was being built, and Harvey Berry, the general manager of a shoe store chain, was looking for talent. I answered his questions in my bib overalls and T-shirt, but he offered me a job. I showed up my first day at Florsheim Shoes in my dad's sport jacket and white tie with a double Windsor knot for full effect and had to be informed that I was overdressed for my job as a stock boy. I was sixteen years old.

I did well in school and graduated early my senior year in January, just a few weeks before I turned eighteen. The morning after my graduation, my new stepmom decided to threaten me with a bucket of water to the face for oversleeping while she was cleaning, the only day I ever saw her clean. She really was a wicked stepmother. That was the last day I woke up in the family home. By the end of the day, I had my own place and was living on my own a few days after turning eighteen.

I thrived at Florsheim. That first store was brand new, and it smelled like leather and newly installed carpet. The merchandise looked and felt luxurious, and the lighting in the new store was mesmerizing to a kid whose playroom was a coal bin. I took every opportunity to advance, took other opportunities to work in stores that needed salespeople or windows trimmed. I even put in time off the clock, much to Dad's chagrin. He would tell me, "Boy, why you doing that shit for free? If you show up for work, get paid for it." Dad had a fixed mindset around being paid for each hour he worked, and my commission-based career path didn't make much sense to him.

Sales were a natural fit for me, and I was never one to pass up an opportunity or a contest to win. Only thirty days after my eighteenth birthday and less than two months after graduating from high school, I was already a manager.

CHAPTER TWO

The Start of a Dream

> First love is only a little foolishness
> and a lot of curiosity.
>
> —GEORGE BERNARD SHAW

Larry: An Irresistible Opportunity

Even back in the 1970s, it was unusual for an eighteen-year-old to find himself in a genuine career, but that's what I found with Florsheim's shoe stores. My willingness to work extra hours, sometimes off the clock, was a major contributor to my success and opportunity for promotion.

The general manager for the St. Louis region then was named Norm Friend. Norm surprised me with three opportunities, but I could only choose one—and I was given only two hours to make up my mind. I was offered the role as a Florsheim general manager in one of three cities: Houston, Texas; Walla Walla, Washington; or San Jose,

California. I had 120 minutes to make one of the biggest decisions of my life. Under the gun, I called Dad at GM and had them pull him off the line so I could ask him whether I should take the job and head west. He told me, "Son, you need to make that decision for yourself." He was never confident Florsheim was treating me well. Yet, he never said yes or no, keeping his influence to himself, letting me find my own way.

I knew Houston to be unnaturally hot and crowded. I imagined Walla Walla would be a wet place where it rained a lot and was dreary. Then there was California! San Jose was close to the Bay Area and was a top area for weather and things to do. Lake Tahoe, San Francisco, and even Disneyland were within a day's drive or less.

The only other influence to consider was a girl I'd met earlier that year. I thought there could be something there, but I wasn't certain she felt the same way about me as I did about her, and so I headed to California. With the song "Do You Know the Way to San Jose?" playing in my head, I packed up my Pontiac Grand Prix and headed west to run the seven stores in the San Jose region.

Sharon: The Co-Ed

I was eighteen years old when I moved into the low rent co-op, Stratford House, in the fall, the same week that the king of rock and roll died in 1977. Elvis's death was definitely big news, but it didn't compare to the reality that I had made it—I was living away from home for the first time; it was exciting. But with a curfew and a chore board, involved house parents, and some very religious roomies, my new life included limits I had to learn to navigate.

The Baptist church next door ran Stratford House. I lived with twenty-eight other girls, and together we shared meals, showers, all the house chores, and a dormitory where we slept in bunk beds with no heat or AC, and where windows were left ajar year-round to meet health codes. In those northern Illinois winters, the large room was a frigid expanse of evenly spaced bodies. Most were able to afford cozy electric blankets; some just shivered.

Groups of four or five girls shared smaller rooms where our dressers and clothes lived, and we might have a couch or a couple chairs, and a desk if there was room. Every semester we were assigned to a committee: maintenance, kitchen, cleaning, spiritual/social, shopping, etc. Every week there was a new schedule posted for the more routine duties like cooking, prayer leaders, and dreaded wake-up duty. We had no alarm clocks in the dorm, which meant there were personal waker-uppers who would whisper, tap, or for the heavier sleepers, shake you awake at your desired time per a chart outside the dorm. It was no more fun to shake a relative stranger awake than be shaken awake by one, but we had to get used to it quickly.

Three showers were shared by nearly thirty girls, and the space was communal in every way. But even with the curfews and bans on beer and boys (without approval and appointments), I still had more freedom than I had at home.

On campus I took my classes and worked hard on my academics. In between classes and my house duties, I occasionally went out to the local bars and frat parties with some of the girls from Stratford. We did our best to make curfew and hide the influence when we came back to bed.

That first semester was a whirlwind of academics and socializing, and I was so relieved and excited when I went back home for Christmas in Belleville, Illinois, hanging out with my BFF, Barb, who had also started her new post–high school life. Together again, we savored our newfound adulthood and freedom. In high school she'd begun working at the mall at a women's clothing store called 5-7-9. She was now a manager there, making her way up the noncollegiate ladder—and making lots of new friends along the way.

Barb had taken up bowling and was in a Friday night league with a bunch of her new friends from the mall. When I arrived there that first time, she was exuberant—the life of the party. Christmas spirits were high that night, and so was the bar tab. We eventually moved from the lanes to the bar and kept the beers going until closing time.

In the parking lot at the night's end, I found myself talking to a guy named Larry. As the group was breaking up to head home, and before I even had time to think about it, I was kissing him, then following him home to his own apartment. We had great chemistry, and we had fun, but I was going back to school in January with no expectations of ever seeing him again, unaware that I'd met my future on Christmas vacation.

Larry: 'Tis the Season

Florsheim shaped my leather-lined workday, but the brand-spanking-new mall was my portal to a social life. All the new shops and restaurants were exciting for a young person who had never journeyed up the new interstate 64. I was content going to Dog and Suds when money was flush, Steven's hardware for a model car, or Zabawa's Grocery for my Suzy Q and RC Cola fix after cutting a few lawns—until I met my first mall. A filet o' fish from Mickey D's was an unknown delight in my youngest years, and I also took full advantage of the food court in the mall.

And I made so many friends—the girls across the way at the 5-7-9 dress shop and the guys at Regal Shoes and others around the mall all got together after work, joining bowling leagues and going bar hopping.

Christmas time at a mall, especially in 1977 when malls were new and shiny, was a true mad rush. The decorations were elaborate at the mall compared to our aging six-foot aluminum tree and kaleidoscope light that projected upon it at my childhood home in Washington Park. That tree seemed like a child's toy compared to the soaring trees and greenery swags filling the soaring heights of the mall.

While working at Florsheim's, I met John and Jim from Regal Shoes, and those guys were always dressed to the T and had the newest fashion in shoes and suits. My pal Keith from the Tinderbox, another store in the mall, was a big guy and brought a unique pipe fragrance to any event. Then there were the ladies from 5-7-9 dress shop, including a girl named Barb, as well as the Claire's boutique gals who were always present at social gatherings. The energy of the season was fueled with youth, promise, and an innocent love of life.

We were hardworking young people who had plenty of steam to blow off after hours of catering to shoppers during the most demanding time of the year. The guys and I would use that huge parking lot at St. Clair Square Mall spinning donuts in our cars whenever snow fell. Our only caution at that young age was avoiding the light poles sprinkled around the lot.

Barb was a ton of fun in a little package. One night at the bowling alley, where our crowd spent a lot of time after work, she brought along an old friend.

When I first met Barb's friend, I mistook her for a different friend Barb had mentioned before, named CP, short for Cheri P. I spoke to Sharon several times through the night before I realized she was not CP. Sharon was different from the other girls in that she was self-assured in her opinions, and outside attitudes didn't affect her.

She was a four-year university girl, unlike the local two-year junior college girls with whom I seldom associated. I was a working stiff who socialized with working women peers and didn't hang out with college girls often.

After a fun night of bowling and drinking, Sharon and I ended up back at my studio apartment, where the festive mood continued. Of course, my Florsheim deco furniture was the talk of the evening. My extra seating was a Florsheim display chair and an extremely used footstool I had repaired. Two wooden crates from an abandoned display window were the extent of my furnishings. On one crate was my nineteen-inch color TV, and upon the other my brandy decanter and snifter held place of pride. My first offering to Sharon was a taste of the brandy (Wild Turkey), which she accepted. The pullout sofa was the comfort area and helped to get the sparks to fly. However, I knew she was going back to school, and I was going back to work the next day.

Sharon: Let the Good Times Roll

I went back to school after Christmas break, but it was so cold and nowhere near as fun as the good times I had with Barb and her welcoming group. I worked two jobs, getting up early to prep food in the residence halls on campus and working for a photographer, taking "party pics" at the fraternities and sororities on campus, hustling proof sheets to get photo orders, and manning the desk and phones in the afternoons. This was the late '70s and well before digital anything, so party pics were one way to document college fun for a lot of folks.

Between classwork and my chores at the Stratford House, I was beyond busy, but whenever I could, I took the train south from school on the weekends to meet Barb and my ever-growing circle of friends for a couple days of fun before heading back to school on Sunday.

Often, I stayed at Barb's house and didn't always let my parents know I was back in town. Even in high school, Barb's mom conspired with us to protect my freedom. She had six kids, Barb being the fourth, and my mom's overprotective nature made no sense to her. She simply saw it as unnecessary, so even if Barb and I were out on the town, her mom would tell my mother that we were upstairs asleep when she called to check up on me.

And no matter what time we got in, Barb's parents were asleep in bed. When I missed curfew at home, often I found my mom frantically cleaning until I was home. I still remember coming home from a fun night out to find the contents of our kitchen drawers spewed out on the floor midway through her reorganization. It seemed kinder to both of us for me to keep my mom in the dark, believing I was away at college, not in town with friends. It would have been even worse for her to know that when I wasn't sleeping over with Barb's family, I was hooking up with that bowling alley guy.

As our new friendship blossomed, Larry began driving up to campus with a friend to bring me home for the weekend. Ultimately, I spent more weekends back in Belleville than I did at Stratford House. In between visits Larry and I exchanged many, many phone calls.

It's hard to conceive in today's cell phone culture, but Stratford House had only one phone, tucked in a beautiful, crafted wood booth in the middle of the second-floor hallway, and I nestled in there with my legs tucked up around me and the door closed, talking about friends and planning visits and dreaming dreams together. Larry sometimes sent me money to settle my long-distance phone bill, and often he was the one who called. When he called me, he'd have to wait for some other girl to hunt me down and for me to get to the phone or for her to return empty-handed. We got to know each other over the course of those weeks, and we saw each other enough to keep things interesting.

As my freshman year came to an end, I seemed to be split between two lives. My college life didn't feel solid, because I didn't quite fit in. I did not live in the residence halls where I worked; I was not in a sorority like the girls I photographed. Though I lived in their co-op, I wasn't a Baptist or even deeply religious at the time. And I was a female in a male-dominated academic program. Though I would see the rare girl in the building where my lectures were held, there were none in my classes with me.

When I struggled with a physics course my sophomore year, I approached the teaching assistant for support. He told me he couldn't help me, and I should just switch majors. It might have been just one guy's opinion, but it felt like common consensus that engineering was not a major for girls.

Lucky for me the Baptist church also ran a boys' co-op directly across the street from the church, and I found myself palling around with Scott, a hog farmer who was studying agricultural engineering. Along with some of the other engineering majors who lived at the boys' house, he was a huge help to me as I struggled with the math and physics classes. Without their help, I would have failed some of my classes. And even though Scott and the other boys were kind, they confirmed my intuition by sharing that engineering was a very competitive field where no one helped each other much. Needing help—and even worse, asking for help—was seen as a weakness.

Ultimately, I was on my own, exploring everything all the time. Academics were a challenge but fulfilling. I still loved everything about school, from lecture halls to chemistry labs to finals week. Stratford House was limiting but allowed me to explore my faith in new ways.

I regularly attended Baptist and nondenominational services when I was in town, met for weekly Bible studies, and learned new ways to pray. I was privileged to live with the most varied group of girls aspiring to become sign-language teachers, lawyers, nutritionists, horticulturists, physical therapists, veterinarians, and more. They were involved in sports and politics and churches and volunteer groups.

College life and college friends were interesting, but it all seemed to compete with my alternate life, the one that was budding with Barb, Larry, and our friends, where I was finding another side of myself.

Larry: Reach Out and Touch Someone

Sharon stayed at my little studio apartment sometimes when she came to town on the weekends. We had fun when she was there, slipping out late at night to pick up bacon at the local 7-Eleven convenience store and frying it up in the earliest hours before the sun came up, filling the tiny studio apartment with that familiar smell and plenty of smoke. Sometimes we fell asleep snuggling and would be startled by her mom's call. *Where is my daughter?* Rose was not a fan of our late nights. I would drop Sharon off and attempt the final kiss of the evening while the porch lights were flashing at an extreme rate. Time was up and our date was at an end.

When Sharon returned to school, I worked at Florsheim. When I called her at the Stratford House, I might spend ten minutes, or three dollars, waiting for her to come pick up the phone or for the girl who answered the phone to come back only to say Sharon was at work. I was not a happy camper when that occurred, and it made it hard to tell if she even wanted to talk to me. I wondered a lot if she felt the same way I did.

I remember sending her roses on Valentine's Day after our first encounter at the bowling alley, but her appreciation fell short of my expectations for a twenty-dollar gift, which was discouraging. But I remained optimistic and continued to woo her over the phone and a couple visits to Champaign until we became somewhat of an item.

Sharon: Man on the Floor

When Larry would visit me at the co-op, a chorus of "man on the floor" rang out through the house. It was quaint but also odd that such a large house was so constrained and dedicated to the social norms of my mom's generation. The summer of love had taken place more than ten years before, and here I was celebrating relationship milestones (once referred to as pining) with candle-passing ceremonies akin to 1950. The juxtaposition of the freedom I found with Barb and in Larry's tiny studio apartment with a pullout sofa bed against the expansive but restrictive Stratford House drove me back to my friends more and more often.

When summer came it felt like being paroled from someone else's life. I got a job as a cashier and stocking shelves at the local Venture store back home (a chain much like K-Mart back in the day) and begged for as many hours as I could to save more for school in the fall. Free time that summer was spent mostly with my friends and on occasional family trips to the lake.

My family had always boated, beginning with an old wood boat and a thirty-horsepower Evinrude motor my dad rehabbed in the 1960s. Back when I was small, Dad would haul that boat and his family to Crab Orchard on weekends. My mom packed everything but the kitchen sink for those trips. We'd rent a cabin near the lake, one of several in a motel setting. I have a few sharp memories of the motel's small pool with not enough chairs and the funny vibrating bed with not enough quarters.

However, the summer I turned nine, we began boating at a new man-made lake closer to home in Litchfield, Illinois—Lake Lou Yeager. Mom and Dad rented a campsite at Lake Lou every summer where we didn't have any running water or electricity. We bathed in the lake, used a legitimate outhouse, and hoarded propane for camp cooking and lanterns. We dug through slushy coolers and battled mosquitos and summer storms. It was the most and best kind of exhausting a kid can experience, and it was, and remains, a priceless treasure.

Over the years I formed a special circle of friends at Lake Lou, and we saw each other through adolescence and beyond. Somehow, we all held those friendships as apart from our "at home" lives. We didn't bring others into the mix, and the only friend from back home who ever went there with me was Barb, and that was rare. I don't think I ever even invited Barb until after our junior year of high school, and by then we'd been best friends for over two years. In any case, Lake Lou was a special glue that held our family, and my sense of self, together.

The northern woods were full of memory and the magic of kids who saw each other nearly every weekend, every summer, every year for much of their lives. The lake was a place where everything else— friends with their dramas and gossip, the games young people play, the academics, the politics of being a woman in engineering school, and the cold nights in the Stratford House—was all left far behind, and the lake and my lake friends embraced me for who I was, who I had always been. Together we shared so many firsts. Our first heartbreaks, our first wild nights in the water without our suits, the first games of truth or dare. We sped in boats down the lake screaming as loud as we could into the wind, because we could and because no one could hear. We water skied and tubed all day, had dock fights all afternoon, took forever-long boat rides under the starriest night skies. In the middle of the lake, we'd turn off the engine and the lights and lay down the seats and just stare up, bobbing in tiny ripples in the dark, hoping to catch a shooting star and gazing up into all the possibility the world holds. It was like one of those wistful coming-of-age movies, but it was real. Even though I had a "real" life back in the suburbs, something about the lake stripped away all the artificial trappings of that life. Nothing is more real than being with people who accept you for who you are without the fronts we put up in our daily lives. It was heaven.

Even time spent with my parents was better at the lake. Dad taught me how to drive a boat and, more importantly, how to dock a boat. I would wake up early there and join my dad out on the dock. He poured me my first cup of coffee on one of those mornings, and I remember asking for sugar or cream to ease the bitterness. He said, "If you're gonna drink coffee, drink it black or not at all." So, I did, and I always have.

My mom was in her heaven too. Her sister Mary lived in Litchfield and had introduced us to the lake. She camped just down the lake a bit, and mom's other sister, Virginia (the one who lived across the street), would eventually lease the lot just two spots from ours. Those three unlikely campers would spend hours sitting at the water's edge, with a fishing pole nearby, planning meals and sharing memories as only sisters can.

As much as my own guard was let down on the lake, so were my parents'. It's like all of our masks came off, and with the gentle lapping sounds of the waves against the shore, we were exposed in the most beautiful ways. My mom's anxieties and OCD were washed away and her spirit restored in that environment, and my dad responded in kind. All the tensions we carried at home had no place at the lake. It was sacred. It is still sacred.

Larry: Hitting the Road

When Sharon came home for the summer, I was excited to see her more often, save on my gas driving up to get her from school, and get a break on those mounting long-distance bills. We had a blast at my apartment, that tiny space that always smelled like bacon and cigarettes.

One day the whole crew came over; it was an interesting day that stretched into night with young people spilling out the threshold of my studio onto the walkway to my second-floor door. We were drinking and having a good time when I went backward over the iron rail and somehow caught my head between the bars. It was a feat of physics, and there I was hanging upside down with my head stuck in a railing with my drunk friends struggling to free me between laughs. Once freed, I fell into the bushes in front of my downstair neighbor's apartment. Young and drunk, I sprang back from the bushes, shook it off, and rejoined the fray.

Earlier the same day, I was showing Sharon the engine of my car, my new 1976 black Pontiac Grand Prix with a four-hundred-cubic-inch motor. When one of us closed the hood, her fingers were caught between the chassis and the hood. I had to get back inside the car to release the hood latch and free her hand. She wasn't too mad, wasn't hurt badly, and laughed it off, reminding me once more that she was different from the other girls I knew.

The chemistry we found at Christmastime was only growing. Along the way we spent more and more time together. I was only nineteen when I met her, and by twenty I was doing my best to win her over, but I was never sure where I stood with her.

That summer after her freshman year when we were beginning to date, I hoped she would invite me along to her family trips to the lake, but she didn't, and I wondered where things were heading for us. My impression of lake life was as a rite of passage to her inner self and her family. I wondered if she was embarrassed of me or not sure I would be approved by her lake family.

I had only met her parents for brief moments when picking her up or following her mom's demands to return her daughter communicated by the fierce flashing of porch lights. When she wasn't at the lake, and when she carved out some time for me, our relationship became stronger.

When she returned to U of I in the fall for her sophomore year, it seemed that my presence was missed. Phone calls and visits seemed to increase, and I felt more important. But then in the spring of her sophomore year, I was given those two hours to decide whether I was going to stay in Illinois or move to California. Maybe if things with Sharon had been more serious than weekends and phone calls, it would have been a harder choice, but I loved my work, and the opportunity would be a rapid rise. With the new leadership role, I would be making more than my dad, who had been working longer than I'd been living. It seemed like a necessary leap.

Sharon: Building My Life

When I came home that first summer after freshman year, I didn't think too much about building a relationship with Larry, as we were getting to know each other. Fate, however, seemed to pull us together. By end of summer, we were officially "a thing."

I returned to Stratford that fall and winter to spend even more time in that tiny phone booth on the second floor. We wrote each other constantly and kept a countdown of days until we'd see each other again.

Over the same summer Larry and I bonded, my roommate, Val, hooked up with Larry's high school best friend, Karl. There was now added incentive for the three-hour trek back and forth on Interstate 57 my sophomore year.

Larry: California Dreaming

When I left for California, I put my Florsheim furniture and other meager belongings in a U-Haul tow-behind five-by-eight-foot trailer, which I pulled with my Grand Prix. The drive across America was remarkably unremarkable. I was on a mission, and windshield time passed as quickly as the power pole lines.

The call from Norm Friend was on a Friday. Sharon and I discussed my move over that weekend. She was focused on school and didn't appear concerned either way, so by Monday I was loaded and on my way to San Jose.

Maybe it happened too fast for them to react, but I don't recall much excitement from my parents or friends other than they had a new place to visit on vacation, and they all followed through—several visited over that summer. Barb was excited to go on an adventure, and this was right up her alley. She began planning to tag along on my drive west, and after a few hours on Sunday, we were both loaded and ready to head out.

The trip itself was uneventful; the real adventure began when I pulled into the city of San Jose and arrived at my swank new crib. I genuinely believed I had arrived. I still recall someone's 1970 Rolls-Royce Silver Shadow next to my covered parking space.

Barb and I agreed I had arrived in a different and exciting world. Everything was new, evidenced by the small trees, clean concrete, and sparkling apartment facades. We walked down the sidewalk to the recreation center and were introduced to the management person who granted my key and the privilege of living in this magical place.

Barb and I wandered around inspecting the amenities in the rec center, and I marveled how far I had journeyed from the farm, liquor store, and paper routes of my younger years. God had blessed my journey. My parents' example of hard work and helping others was paying off big in my own young life.

Even though I was thousands of miles away, Sharon and I kept calling each other. She was finishing up sophomore year and agreed to visit sometime during the summer break.

My apartment was a bachelor pad. I didn't even have a real bed until Sharon arrived and we bought one. The furnishings were the same retired Florsheim floor pieces, and though the apartment was spacious, it was sparse. The amenities were great though—there was a real pool, not like the grungy indoor pool at my studio apartment back home. The weather was beautiful, and my best girl was getting to see my work paying off and experience my new life firsthand.

I was twenty-one years old managing seven stores from San Jose, and I was on top of the world.

Sharon: When You're Gone

Our circle of friends was a little dazed when Larry accepted the job in California in the spring of 1979. After all these years, I can't recall the specifics, but I'm confident there were tears and beers all around at a farewell extravaganza of some kind. We'd grown so comfortable with each other, in our gang of friends, and in the routine of long-distance dating.

We'd made so many memories over that first year, dancing the nights away in country-western bars and disco dens. The long calls and late nights in Larry's apartment talking and dreaming together were cherished. Still, he left that March, making the drive with Barb riding shotgun—and making new memories without me.

I finished my sophomore year and went home for one last summer in Belleville. The unwelcoming and challenging engineering program had worn on me, and I decided to switch majors, from engineering to hospital dietetics. This change required more biology, so I enrolled in two courses at the local junior college that summer. The classes were short term, and the double coursework was just what I needed to keep my mind busy before I finally visited Larry in California in August. The calls hadn't ended just because he left Illinois, but we weren't sure where the relationship was going. So, we needed some time together to figure it out.

CHAPTER THREE

For Better or Worse

> If we will be quiet and ready enough, we shall
> find compensation in every disappointment.
>
> —HENRY DAVID THOREAU

Sharon: Golden State of Mind

My youthful independence was only enhanced by my first trip to California to see Larry at the end of summer 1979. The trip was an adventure. I had never been west of Missouri, never traveled so far alone, and never spent two weeks with Larry alone. His California apartment was so different from the one in Belleville and yet somehow just the same. He had a bedroom now, instead of just a pullout couch, but the only furniture was a single bed and some dinged and disused Florsheim floor pieces. He had picked up a couch along the way and placed a crate in front of it as a coffee table.

Not that we ever used it, but Larry now had an actual kitchen with a full-sized refrigerator. The dining room set was a round display table from the store surrounded by four chairs for seating customers to try on shoes. I loved it all because it was just us and, in hindsight, the first place we'd call home together. The complex was beautiful, with a real pool and clubhouse, not the dingy indoor basement pool from his last place. The weather was pure California, without the humidity from back home, warm days and crisp nights even in August.

When Larry had come home earlier that summer to visit, we were surrounded by our usual crowd, but of course he no longer had his own place where we could retreat. We went from staying together on occasion in March, to a long-distance relationship, to awkward visits that were more social engagements than private interactions. So, when I arrived in California and could spend time with Larry, and just Larry, it was a whole new world for us both.

Larry took time to show me around and make some day trips down Highway 101 and to Fisherman's Wharf. The sightseeing was exciting, but being reunited and having time alone to talk and touch was so much better than Disneyland.

When I returned home at the end of August for my junior year at the University of Illinois, my heart ached. We had called each other a lot before he moved to California, but now we were talking as often as we could afford to and sending letters, sometimes three in one week. I was eager to get through the year so I could spend the full summer of 1980 in California.

Larry: Every Time You Go Away

The first time Sharon visited me in California was my chance to show off my new home. I saved up my vacation to spend time with Sharon and take her to visit San Francisco and Fisherman's Wharf. I was never much of a seafood guy back home, but the clam chowder was extraordinary, and I loved sharing that experience with Sharon. We went to Disneyland together, and it was a world apart from the Six Flags over MidAmerica, just outside St. Louis.

Coming from the Midwest, I had never experienced anything like Lake Tahoe. Climbing the mountain was exciting. However, entering the town of Lake Tahoe and seeing the lake was breathtaking. Showing all of this to Sharon made it more magical for me too, but I knew she wasn't going to stay.

From the night we met, I always knew school was important to Sharon. Her dedication and focus were some of the many reasons I loved her. Her independent spirit relieved my own sense of responsibility, as I knew that if we ended up together, she would be a true partner with similar goals and ambitions. Though I didn't relish her absence or look forward to the long-distance bills that would follow her return to college, I never doubted she was worth waiting for.

Like I always have, I kept busy with work. I found myself buying into the California lifestyle and making friends in San Jose. All the amenities and conveniences appealed to me, but I had reservations about the work ethic I saw at the mall, specifically with some of my employees at the store.

I liked California being laid back, but during work hours it didn't feel quite right. I quickly learned that, unlike back home, in San Jose no one questioned a mall-based barter system. I could use my limited but healthy store discount to buy a nice pair of shoes to trade with another mall employee for a suit. However, I was never completely satisfied that those making trades actually paid for the products they were swapping or followed the policies of their own stores.

Even more concerning, I suspected some of my own employees were accustomed to trading shoes they hadn't bought before I took over the store. I faced a constant challenge disciplining my coworkers. Theft was an offense that should lead to termination, but catching an employee stealing from Florsheim was very difficult to prove. Even for lesser infractions, several times written warnings were issued and signed by a witness and a coworker only for the notice to disappear before it was sent to headquarters in Chicago.

One of the reasons I was brought in from the Midwest was the work ethic and integrity established by leadership in the St. Louis area. I was in San Jose less than a year before my regional profitability had reversed course from a significant loss to a gain. Based upon the profitability I led and my agreement with leadership, I was looking forward to over $10,000 in bonuses at the end of 1980.

Even as a kid, I was always looking for what happens if I meet or exceed your expectations. Even in my earliest days of my career, I had a knack for understanding and achieving the goals necessary for success. With my work performance and turning the store around, I felt like the world was my oyster in California.

Sharon: Staying the Course

My friend Val had been my roommate and best friend at Stratford House. In my junior year, we found a small apartment off campus. Karl drove up a lot to visit Val, and we still went south a lot of weekends. Since I changed my major and bolstered my biology credits over the summer, I was in different lecture halls with new people. It should have been exciting, because I had made a big decision and done the work for it in the accelerated summer classes, but I couldn't get California off my mind. I made a few trips back, with Larry buying the airfare, for Thanksgiving and spring break. Larry was home that year some too, so we just kept the countdowns going.

I remained as focused on my schooling as I could. I loved my new major, and the courses were challenging but applicable and fun. Food science and biochemistry were my favorites. In my third year of college, I seemed to have more stability than the previous years. I was no longer in Stratford House, and I still had my circle of friends with Barb back in Belleville. I missed Larry, but between school and an active social life paired with our letters and phone calls, I got through it. Knowing that when summer came we would be together again made it easier to be apart.

Both of Us: Two Tickets to Paradise

We reunited at the airport train station in early June 1980 and were inseparable for the summer. We even worked at two different shoe stores in the same mall, just across the hallway from each other. Our breaks were even spent together at Florsheim.

When we weren't working, we lazed around at Larry's apartment or explored the area. Larry was playing baseball in a men's league, and we had befriended the downstairs neighbor, Bob. He was a Californian who was fresh off a breakup with the love of his life. He subsequently had "Lonesome Loser" on some kind of loop and played it at max volume so that our floors thumped, and the words became ingrained in our memory bank for life. We shared dinners and played cards when he was not too sad for company.

In our Florsheim-chic decor, we were two peas in a pod, enjoying the togetherness and "just-us-ness" of every day. It seemed perfect in those early days in California; we were so young and inexperienced, growing closer with the passing weeks. We were content with whatever came our way.

We didn't spend too much time at home that summer though. We frequently went to the beach or trekked to Lake Tahoe for exploring, partying, and gambling. It quickly became our favorite destination, and each time we went we talked about the possibility of living there one day. Though we had known each other for nearly three years and most of our relationship had been long-distance, it felt like we'd been a couple forever. Everything we did—every touch and every glance—carried innuendo of growing closer, growing together.

Unfortunately, the summer could not last forever, and the University of Illinois awaited Sharon's return. The last night we spent together in California, Larry wrote a letter letting Sharon know how much that summer meant to him. We both knew that our love would survive separation and accepted the reality that if you really love someone, you can set them free to follow their dreams and honor their commitments to themselves. Larry was committed to success with Florsheim, and Sharon was committed to her independence and finishing school. We would also soon realize that living out this belief isn't easy.

Sharon: See You in September

When I returned to the University of Illinois, I had to reapply to Stratford since Val's dad had bought her and her sister a small house to share, as her sister had joined us on campus. My mom and dad had paid for my tuition, and I was determined to finish school and have a career before any boy or man would take a permanent place in the picture.

I'd moved in, signed up for classes, bought books, and was only a day or two into classes before I realized that I could not stay in Champaign without Larry. We'd been apart only two weeks, and I'd read his letter repeatedly. I had no idea I could be so in love until I couldn't function and couldn't stop crying for no reason, regardless of where I was in my day. I had no idea that it could hurt, physically hurt, this way, to just be apart from someone. Every part of my being, heart and mind, body and soul, needed to get back to California to continue the beginning of the rest of my life. I knew I could go to college in California. I knew I could still graduate, but I couldn't spend another year so far from the love of my life.

I made a fast plan to get a refund for my mom from the bursar and withdrew from the university. My father was a railroad employee, but even with his discount, it was less expensive to fly to San Francisco than to take the train. I returned to Belleville and told my parents I was heading west. Dad was accepting, but when I boarded the train from Belleville to Chicago to catch that plane, my mom was beside herself that I was leaving Illinois and had no known plans to return. Later in life I would understand that her heart was probably aching even more than mine in that moment. My heart ached for a boy; hers ached for a child, and I would not understand the vast difference for many years.

Both of Us: Reunited

Sharon arrived in California a second time that year, and the apartment was no longer Larry's apartment, but it became our home. Sharon found work easily again, taking a job at the café next to Florsheim, which complemented the food science curriculum she'd taken on after switching her major as well as her history of customer service work.

Early on we discussed San Jose State College and how important it was to us as a couple for Sharon to continue and complete her education. We knew that marriage and kids were a no-go until Sharon had finished school, and that was fine for both of us. That fall and the onset of winter were entirely magical. We were alone together, and we had the whole world ahead of us.

We resumed our adventures in San Francisco and even drove all the way down Highway 101 to one of Larry's regional Florsheim stores in Salinas—then on to Monterey, Carmel-by-the-Sea, Hearst Castle, and finally Disneyland. We explored as much of California as we could in those four months. Our favorite spot, however, was a happy accident.

Coming from the Midwest, neither of us was bothered by snow. However, we were not used to the hulking mountains of Northern California and the Nevada border. One afternoon drive to Lake Tahoe became a nighttime journey when the wind picked up and the snow came down harder than we'd ever seen. The orange highway markers rose several feet above a tunnel of six-foot snowdrifts on either side of the road.

We came upon the snow chain turnout at the twin bridges and had to decide to pay extortioner's prices for tire chains or turn around and stop at the Strawberry Lodge several miles below. Even had we bought chains, fate had her mind made up for us, as soon after we turned around, the mountain pass to Tahoe closed completely.

What might have seemed like a huge disappointment at best and a natural disaster leaving us to the mercies of the road at worst turned into a magical morning. In the dark December night, we found our way on the west side of the pass to the quaint little cottage sweetly named the Strawberry Lodge.

Coming into the inn from the cold and tense drive, we were greeted by a log fire, the fragrant smoke and warmth against the cold blizzard air providing a sensory experience that was like nothing either of us had ever experienced. The place embraced us with its cozy feel and immediately felt familiar and new all at once.

The entrance hall is something we will never forget, and though our room itself wasn't terribly memorable, the next morning is a memory we will share for the rest of our lives together. We awoke to the silent aftermath of a blizzard, gently disrupted by the close sounds of running water. We went to the window and together beheld the extraordinary beauty of the river rushing through the glistening expanse of snow. The early morning light was spectacular, but not yet glaring.

We snuggled in our room that morning, so grateful for the beauty of the blizzard, for our togetherness, and for the circumstances that allowed us this moment and the promise of more to come.

Before 1980 was over, we were engaged. Sharon's mom gave her a diamond that we had set into a ring. We were working, living, and loving our life together in California. The winter holidays were approaching, and the New Year loomed full of promise.

Larry: When the Bottom Drops Out

Back at work, I continued to struggle with employees who didn't want to do any job that wasn't "their job," and this attitude was tricky for someone like me who started as a stock boy. I heard rumblings of union activity and made sure my supervisor back East knew what was going on and sought his advice. I was twenty-one, hardly a union buster, and I needed guidance and support. Despite the attitudes that were prevalent in San Jose, I was still able to turn the stores around and did my best to keep morale up while making our stores profitable.

I was surprised when I was called to the Fairmont Hotel in San Francisco by a vice president of Florsheim from Chicago and the corporate lawyer. Instead of training and supporting me as an ambitious young manager willing to work hard and do what was right, they grilled me about the union activity for nearly five hours before releasing me for loss of control of the San Jose area. My supervisor in Chicago was knowledgeable of all the union activity; however, I assume he was protecting himself or was not disclosing fully all the facts. Plus, the added bonus of $10,000 they no longer needed to pay to fulfill my agreement was a great incentive to write me off. The nearly two years of success I had making Florsheim's stores profitable after losing money before I came didn't matter. What mattered was the whiff of union activity and the perceived costs to efficiency and operations.

The one satisfying event of losing my job was that my supervisor at corporate had to insert himself in the mess they had created. I had asked for help; however, it fell upon deaf ears. The agitators looking for unionization were promoted to management positions so they could no longer organize, and their previous jobs were staffed by part-time Florsheim loyalists who could not pass a union vote. The reaction was harsh, swift, and not debatable.

I had risen to the top of my career field quickly but went in a free fall with no net. I spent days looking for a new career thinking it would be easy, as a young man with my talents would be in high demand. Oops! Was I surprised that a twenty-two-year-old man with no college experience or degree, now unemployed with no references, and experienced in a limited sales field, would not be employable. I do recall applying with a new company looking for an inventory control specialist—it was called Apple Computers. Unfortunately, they were not looking for someone who could look at a row of shoeboxes and say there were 168 pairs on that wall. Several jobs selling insurance were available; however, it was a limited salary with a draw/commission, and you earned as you went. My savings were limited, because I had been looking forward to that big bonus at the end of the year.

After a night in a five-star hotel, I had to drive back to our home in San Jose and let Sharon know that my job was mine no longer. She was starting classes the next month, and I was looking for my next job.

Sharon: Paradise Lost

When Larry told me he was fired by Florsheim, my heart broke for him. I was not attached to his job, his income, or anything but Larry himself. The pain of losing his position and the bonus he had worked so hard to earn seemed inconsolable at first and was so unfair. Our work always defines us to some degree, and leaving a job for any reason is never easy, especially when you've spent significant time with a company and given so much. Larry had grown up at Florsheim, and it was a tough blow to be let go over something he couldn't control. But, Larry being Larry, despite the pain and the anger about what happened, he didn't hesitate to look for a new job. He was always so ambitious and motivated. He loved working, and he was not satisfied to accept failure. I saw his vulnerability and his strength in this difficult time.

For me, however, I was going to school, whether in California or in Illinois. We wanted to stay in California because we were so happy there, but the early '80s heralded a terrible economy and great difficulty finding management or senior positions in the competitive area where we lived. Café work wasn't hard to find, but Larry wasn't like me. I relished food science and the logistics of food service. He loved strategy and improving processes to make businesses thrive. We each had our passions, but his vision for his life couldn't be found in California in 1981.

I wasn't going to stay in California without Larry. He was my reason for heading west, and I would return to Illinois with him too. Larry and I gave up our little apartment and the Golden State and went back home. He found a small apartment on Main Street in Belleville, and we spent Christmas readjusting and anticipating next moves. I still needed to graduate and ended up going alone back to Champaign in January to start my senior year over again, gratefully moving in with Val and her younger sister in the house off campus that her dad had bought. It would be better to be a couple of hours apart than a couple of time zones apart, but it wasn't easy.

I spent the earliest days of 1981 shivering in my little makeshift bedroom that was actually a screened porch on the back of Val's little house. We closed off the glass-shuttered windows with plastic and threw in a twin bed and an old chest of drawers. I didn't even have room to walk; I could just shuffle alongside the wall-to-wall furniture. I had to walk through Val's bedroom to get to my room, so I pre-planned most days to bring out what I "might" need later to avoid interrupting her sleep schedule and Karl's frequent visits. Somewhat enclosed, it wasn't technically outdoors, but it was even colder than the Stratford House, with its windows open year-round, had ever been. We were so far off campus that to get to class or to work I had to ride a bike or take a bus. On the coldest days in Champaign, I had to choose between spending money on the bus and having money to buy myself food. I was a long, long way from the cozy fire of the Strawberry Lodge or the hours of cuddling we'd spent on our apartment couch.

It was a tough semester, financially and emotionally, but even then I was so grateful for a friend to help me through. I believe God puts people in our lives who are His great army of angels, and Val was, and remains, an angel in my world.

So, ever stubborn, as my mom would say, like my dad before me, I was not going to quit school. Even if I wasn't so close to finishing my degree, I knew I would finish. Even if I hated that porch bed arrangement, even if I sloshed that bike through snow and rain, even if I couldn't contribute to the grocery fund, I knew I would finish. I spent my childhood watching my mother and her generation struggle with their financial dependence on husbands who may or may not honor their obligations. As cold, lonely, and hungry as I might have been, I would never find myself dependent on anyone else. I loved Larry, and I would always love Larry, but I never wanted to be a burden to him or to sell myself short.

I didn't want to work, because I wanted freedom to commute to Belleville on weekends or be available when Larry came for visits. I investigated student loans but didn't take any. I had plans to work at a hospital in Belleville that summer, working in their food service and observing the dietitians, to help my résumé in hopes of gaining an internship after graduation, as an internship was required to become a registered dietitian. I could survive one tough semester with the promise of summer back home with Larry to look forward to.

Larry: Back on the Horse

It was time to pack up and return home. Never had I failed at such a high level. I was so young and so proud of my ability to achieve success. However, in a few hours in San Francisco, I was leveled to a nobody. Realizing my options for a new career were few and far between, Sharon and I loaded the Grand Prix with the same five-by-eight-foot trailer and headed back to Illinois. The drive started as poorly as my career had ended, with fog so heavy in the Fresno Valley that we had to detour after only a few hours on the road.

A few days later, before Christmas, we arrived at my dad's apartment after he had left for work around six thirty in the morning. After driving all night, I was intensely hungry. I opened the freezer and grabbed the bacon wrapped in aluminum foil, only to be surprised by hundred-dollar bills stacked inside. I had heard of cold cash but had never seen it in this form.

Dad was in the middle of a divorce with my short-term stepmom, and this was where his assets were literally frozen. I had seen it all but was not surprised by his actions. He had worked all his life, and his thirty-five years of hard work were not to be sacrificed for his two years of marriage to this crazy lady. It seemed we were all starting over.

With the support of Sharon and my dad, and the resiliency my parents taught me, I came to understand that starting over was a challenge and did not make me as a person a complete failure. I didn't have California money, but I did have a small nest egg and was able to secure a one-bedroom apartment on West Main Street in Belleville. I was a couple miles from my dad and from Sharon's parents.

Most of our relatives were close by, and my support group was solid. The challenge with returning was not having a job and only a small amount of expendable money. Prior to the Florsheim disaster, I was always employed. Things like the phone, power, and apartment bills were no longer easy, and I had to be creative to get my new affairs in order.

Only knowing shoes was a challenge when looking for a new career. My unemployment check was based on my salary in California, which was $240 per week, and the job pool was shallow. I had two choices: lower my expectations and/or accept less income. I was never one to sit idly by and wait.

I always heard success is about who you know, not what you know. Wrong again, young Larry! I finally agreed with my dad that maybe I should be at the General Motors plant and get paid for every minute I worked. Inflation was high, and jobs were hard to come by. So, I asked Dad, and he said they were only hiring college kids. Even though my dad and my uncle Larry didn't need college degrees, my generation required them for the same jobs. So, I had to think about my education.

It wasn't that I was too proud to go back to school, but when I entered the line to start the process and saw thirty people in front of me, I realized it was no different from the job market itself. I turned around and went home. I was either overqualified because of my previous salary or underqualified from an educational standard.

I paged through newspapers daily looking for my next career and continued to come up empty-handed. One of my past assistant managers at Florsheim heard of my dilemma and said I should check out the rent-to-own (RTO) industry. I had never heard of the term RTO or even understood what the business model was all about. Still, I was excited because an RTO company, Christa Rentals, offered an interview, and that was an opportunity.

During the one-hour interview, I was hired. I was not experienced enough to place as a manager. Instead, I was a candidate for manager in training (MIT), which meant $4.50 per hour or $180 a week. I was collecting $240 a week on unemployment sitting at home watching TV, and I was now required to drive forty miles a day to a location that had not been previously discussed in the interview process. Still, it was an opportunity.

It was a new company in a new industry, both with little to no structure. I was coming from a corporate environment where every T was crossed and every I dotted. How would I survive what came next? Do I continue to work these low wages with a long commute or make a pivot and start a new career path? I chose to show my skills and create success.

By the time Sharon graduated, I had made manager in a six-month window and was being considered an up-and-comer. Being a multi-level manager was next on my agenda.

Sharon: The Graduate

The summer after we got back from California was a summer to remember. Larry had found a job with Christa Rentals. I was making minimum wage at the hospital that summer and moved into his Main Street apartment, and the old gang was back together. Everyone was legal to drink, and we spent endless nights at Bobby's, a country-western bar, appreciating our right to imbibe, while dancing, dancing, dancing. If we weren't there, we were at Fairview Inn, playing pool and lining up spent longneck beer bottles like dominoes in a heated race to create the longest chain. We had drinking games and ongoing bets. There were peppermint schnapps shots and whiskey chasers. Everyone gathered at our apartment regularly before and after hitting the bars for gaming tournaments on Larry's new Atari system.

We spent a weekend at the new hotel next to Six Flags with Barb and her fiancé, Steve, where the kamikaze became our new favorite shot! We partied until sunup on many of those nights, and I had a few mornings I went to work without any sleep, chugging coffee to work a 5:30 a.m. shift. Looking back, we were doing it all wrong but doing it all right. It was the best of times!

Summer ended, and I went back to the University of Illinois for what I thought was my final year. I had full loads and loved the courses and my major. Classes included chemistry of food, advanced biochemistry, quantity food prep, food labs, advanced nutrition—everything was coming together. I decided to put an emphasis on food service management and even loved the required business courses. When spring semester ended in 1982, I was remorseful to find I was one class short of graduation and would need to take an eight-week summer course to finish up. Ever understanding, Val let me stay on the porch a little longer.

To become a registered dietitian, I needed to get accepted into an internship at a teaching hospital, then take my state exam. The internships were insanely competitive, and counselors recommended applying to as many as feasibly possible. I applied to only one. There was only one hospital in St. Louis, the closest major city with a teaching hospital, and I was not going to be separated from Larry any longer. We had been engaged and apart for over a year and a half. It was time to be together. I often wonder how different my life might be had I been accepted to that internship instead of denied. I would not become a registered dietitian, but I still had my degree, and took a job running a nursing home kitchen in Belleville while we started making wedding plans. I would later see this pattern repeat itself—stopping just short of the goal, settling for the good enough—and still struggle to finish strong after all these years.

CHAPTER FOUR

From the Altar to Alabama

> You know you're in love when you can't fall asleep
> because reality is finally better than your dreams.
>
> —DR. SEUSS

Larry: Meet the In-Laws

While Sharon was at school, despite living near them, my path didn't cross with her parents often, until we started to plan the wedding. Early in our relationship, Sharon's mom was not a Larry fan, and her snaggletooth dog, Brutus, liked me even less. Brutus made sure I stayed too uncomfortable to work any kind of charm on Mrs. Koerner.

When Sharon's parents first met me, I was selling shoes at Florsheim, not an occupation they'd imagined for a boyfriend. I also was the guy who delayed their only daughter's education, caused her to jet off to California, and came back unemployed. Now, I was going to marry her, but I had no higher education, and my new career was

59

renting stuff to people who had no credit. I was hardly the ideal son-in-law. But, like all things that matter to me—and nothing mattered to me more than Sharon—I persisted.

Eventually, after taking small bites of the poisoned apple, I made headway. I knew I had arrived when I was finally invited to Lake Lou. Sharon's lake trips had always seemed sacred and mysterious, so when I was finally invited, I felt like I'd won a long race.

The allure of Lake Lou was that it was a treasured part of Sharon's life and one of the few mysteries I was not allowed to share. I wasn't sure if the cold response I got when hinting I would like to go to the lake was due to her mom's negative vibes against me or if it was Sharon's own boundary. Not being sure, it made me feel left out and insecure. I just knew the lake was off limits, so it was a rite of passage for me to be accepted. Either Sharon wore her parents down or they realized we were a real item, and I was going to be in all parts of her life. Either way, I felt I'd finally made it.

After a few visits, I grew to understand the importance of this ritual. Sleeping in the pop-up, with no AC in a balmy ninety-degree night was part of the experience. When I first started the visits, we had to load all the weekend food and supplies into a boat to be motored across the lake. Eventually, we were able to pay for access to the lot across private property, which eliminated the trek up the hill to the platform where everything was stored. Even water had to be fetched and lugged back from the marina. A full five-gallon jug was the minimum daily amount required to keep the coffee, tea, and cooking items going.

Despite the specific and necessary prep work, once at the camp site, weekend life became simple. The wind change would bring in the aroma of the outhouse a few yards away, and to bathe we just grabbed a bar of soap and headed to the lake. If I needed a real shower, I would grab the five-gallon black bag off the dock. It heated during the day and could get me and my hair clean, unlike the muddy lake water. It was perfect, because figuring out hot water and clean hair was simpler and more organic than my life at work. The absence of luxury makes us appreciate the basics and the people who share them with us.

Sharon: Mother Knew Best

Once I accomplished my degree and fulfilled that promise to myself, focus changed to the wedding. Larry and I had lived together in California, and now we were living together again in Belleville, so a big wedding wasn't important to me. I just wanted to be with Larry, and the wedding was icing on that cake.

My mom, however, had other ideas. She had only one daughter, and she was determined to see me walk down the aisle in a white dress, even if the dress was not the pristine symbol she had expected it to be when I was growing up.

The wedding would, of course, be in a Catholic church. This was not negotiable with my mom, and it was a good thing for us that Larry happened to be Catholic too. We met with Father Kuhl at St. Augustine's in Belleville for the official blessing of the Church and to reserve it for our wedding Mass, June 25, 1983. Mom and I secured Fischer's Restaurant for the reception and selected a buffet menu. Fischer's recommended a DJ, and we were quickly halfway through planning. With the date and venues selected, we just needed invitations, flowers, cake, a photographer, and a dress.

One of my high school jobs was working for a florist, so we went there, and the owner happily discounted his beautiful arrangements for the altar, reception tables, bouquets, and boutonnieres. I found my dress instantly on the sale rack at the bridal shop, and it was a perfect fit! Fate was making things easy for me.

Barb was still working at the 5-7-9 women's clothing shop at the mall, so we picked out dresses for bridesmaids from her store. Because I was keen to elope, I wasn't too invested in the bridesmaids' look. We were able to find the right sizes for the bridesmaids in one particular well-priced dress. It happened to be lilac and off the shoulder. It was a dress I would never choose for myself, but I just wanted to marry Larry, not play dress-up with my friends.

Barb came to the rescue, as she called in sizes from other stores and held them in her back room until they went on clearance. This inside connection meant everyone got by affordably with something that wasn't my priority.

Aside from the guest list and getting the invitations mailed, everything came together quickly. The invitation list was over three hundred people, mostly family. Back then we hand addressed, stuffed, stamped, and sealed each invitation at Mom and Dad's kitchen table. For each sealed and stamped envelope, we checked off now-grown-up cousins, lake friends, teammates, classmates, and workmates.

The effects of my mom's leadership and our planning were extraordinary for a couple kids with no savings and only dreams of what was to be. Years later my own daughter would ask if a big wedding was worth the expense, and I assured her it most definitely is. Marking such a big life decision with a celebration like that, where everyone we loved took part, has always been one of my best memories.

Everything fell into place. The beautiful ceremony was followed by the best party of my life. This gift from my parents for Larry and me to begin our lives in a joyful spirit is a treasure. We visited each guest at every table, then danced our hearts out. We stopped long enough to eat and cut the cake, and we danced some more.

Our first dance song was "Can I Have This Dance for the Rest of My Life?" and even if it is a bit cheesy, I love the lyrics still. That song expressed everything my heart was holding at the time and everything I hoped to enjoy in my future.

The father-daughter dance took me right back to all those times I stood on my dad's feet in our living room as a little girl. I can still feel his big rough railroader hand holding mine and the little extra squeeze he gave me all those years ago. With him gone now, that moment was worth all the fuss. All thanks go to my momma for insisting we do it big to do it "right." The wedding would not be the last time that doing something I thought I did not want to do ended up being a huge positive in my life.

If we had eloped, we wouldn't have had those dances with my dad and with Larry. All these years later, I feel closest to Larry when we dance. In particular our song does sometimes come to mind, even now. The lyrics, "Would you be my partner every night? ... when we're together it feels so right," are so appropriate still. He has been a true partner all these years, and it still feels so right—most of the time. But that's marriage, and a beautiful wedding is a memorable way to begin.

Larry: That Magic Moment

Sharon and her mom were planning the wedding, and I wasn't a necessary part of their designs. Leading up to the big day, June 25, 1983, I focused on my career and enjoyed the prospect of marrying Sharon.

Though Sharon's family was highly involved in the logistics, my family wasn't on the hook for anything except the rehearsal dinner. Even though my family was not a huge part of the planning or even the wedding itself, I know most of them were excited to see me so happy. It brought out my dad's protective side. He pulled Sharon aside at a barbeque over the summer and told her that he suspected her of being after my money—not the money I had, but the money he was confident I'd have in the future.

If only he knew the situation bringing me back to Illinois had changed things so substantially. Regardless, my dad always kept faith that I would make a success of my life, and, surely after his horrible second marriage, he wanted better for me on my way to the top. He was proud of me, but men of his generation didn't know how to display affection or share those feelings with their children, even or especially when they were grown. However, his actions spoke where more direct words failed him.

When I was about thirteen years old, Dad said he wished he had ten more ball players like me, because we'd never lose a game. That one statement meant more than any greeting cards or simple utterance ever could. So motivating were his words that I still try to earn his respect while playing senior baseball the last twenty years. That he wanted to know Sharon was good enough for his son says so much, and I'm sure he soon realized she was more than good enough—she was everything I needed to be my best self.

The day finally came. There she stood and began her wedding march—such a beauty! Sharon's dress was perfect for her slight figure. Everything about her was effortlessly exquisite. I knew in that moment how truly blessed I was and am. Here was a human being radiating the rare qualities of beauty, independence, and true love. Each of these things is special, but how rare is it to find them in one person? She was incredible, and she wanted to come here in front of everyone we knew and promise to marry me and be with me for the rest of our lives.

I was a bit punch drunk from the miracle of marrying this extraordinary woman and went into the reception in a state of joy. The reception was incredible, with all our friends and relatives surrounding us to celebrate our love and commitment. I visited with so many people, but I was excited to head off on a cruise to the Bahamas with Sharon for our honeymoon. I credit Sharon's mom for her planning—doves were released, and people still remember our wedding almost forty years later.

On the wedding night, we stayed at the Renaissance Hotel across from the airport and had to park in short-term parking to make our flight the next morning. In 1983 there was no two-hour check-in; maybe we had thirty minutes between checking and boarding. Our bags made it to the cruise ship, and we were simultaneously relieved and giddy when we started our next adventure.

When we got home from the Bahamas, I cringed about how much our parking would be from leaving the car in short term. When the lady asked me for my short-term parking ticket, I asked her what would happen if I lost it. She apologetically said, "I'll have to charge for a whole day," so I gladly agreed to the one-day charge. The difference in that parking charge covered my beer tab from the honeymoon. Married life was looking great!

Sharon: Young Professionals

My first job out of college was food service director at Castlehaven, a small nursing home in Belleville. I was twenty-three years old and managing a staff of twelve, feeding 130 residents three times a day. The responsibilities included noting dietary needs, procuring food, and maintaining equipment. Early on my most difficult task was wrangling staff into food safety compliance and cleaning, cleaning, cleaning.

We tore the place apart in that first month, taking everything that wasn't bolted to the floor out the back door for cleaning and deroaching. We scrubbed ovens and walk-in freezer racks until our biceps ached. Things were changing, and it felt good to make a difference that was so tangible. My lead cook was not on board, however, and it was the first time I had to fire someone. I was afraid because she was boisterous and threatening, storming out with profanity and warnings to watch my back and my tires. Thankfully, nothing ever came of her threats, but getting rid of her led to a better staff. Still, the intensity of her in my tiny office, yelling inches from my face, is a memory that comes to mind whenever I hear the name Rita.

My second job was at a nursing home chain in St. Louis, a big company in a big city with big opportunities. In addition to serving the residents and managing the employees, I worked daily with a registered dietitian. We had so much in common with our academic backgrounds and goals, so we made an amazing team. The job was interesting and challenging, especially as it was largely Jewish occupancy, and we observed the holidays and traditions closely, including kosher kitchen etiquette at certain times of the year. Every time I learned something new, I grew.

The facility where I worked was one of a chain owned by a couple, both highly involved in the day-to-day of the business. The husband was a shrewd businessman who could dole out praise as intensely as he provided cutting criticism. His eye was always on costs and margins. The wife was a Holocaust survivor with a fervor to celebrate life and a keen eye for detail. She was typically kind but employed Gladys, her assistant, to do her bidding. And Gladys was not kind. The three of them didn't enjoy the best communication, which led to conflicts and some confusion on what was expected.

I was responsible for purchasing, but once in a while the husband would take a vendor call or "find a deal," and cases of food would show up unannounced to be worked into the menu and the storeroom. Once, he procured cases of matzo balls, which was great, as Passover seder dinner was coming up. When they were served, the wife could tell they were not the usual, better brand and sent Gladys to set me straight that this brand was never to be used. When I tried to explain that I hadn't bought them, she said it was still my fault, that I should find a way to make both bosses happy! It was a constant push-pull, because she wanted "the best" and he wanted "the bottom line." Gladys, of course, had no advice on how to appease them both.

Yet, they could be extremely generous. While I was there, they hosted the most beautiful baby shower for me, celebrating so fully the life growing inside of me. Their reverence was inspiring, but the nursing home was not the best place for me to grow my career. I wanted to go further in management, and I was willing to go back to school and work hard to make that happen. However, over time I knew my elbows weren't sharp enough and my personality wasn't caustic enough to push my way to the top at this company, so I found a new opportunity. I took huge management experience with me and a new confidence in my ability to build a team environment and improve operations. The most important thing I took with me was the knowledge that having two bosses could make life hell, especially a husband-wife team—a lesson I never forgot.

Larry: Begin Again

Starting over in the rent-to-own space was easier than I expected it to be. Soon, my compliance background regarding policies and procedures was recognized and valued. I didn't realize my corporate background and structure would be needed in this groundbreaking industry, but it was. Understanding the numbers always came easily for me, and I brought many efficiencies that kept cheaters from taking advantage of me and the company.

I progressed quickly in the workplace and once again produced several managers. Eventually, I was recognized for getting things accomplished and went beyond the single store where I was assigned. I traveled and did whatever was asked of me.

After all these years, one of my regrets is how I worked from seven in the morning to seven at night every day, and I couldn't help Sharon as much as she needed early in our marriage. Once promoted to general manager, I opened more than thirty new stores from Tampa, Florida, to the Carolinas to Madison, Wisconsin. Many times I'd leave on Monday and return on Saturday.

Installing carpet, building TV displays, and assembling counters were never beneath me. It never occurred to me that carpentry work may not be in my job description; I just did it because it needed to be done. Looking back on it, I realize I always had an entrepreneurial approach to work and to life.

I built value in the company by opening new stores and generating profitable revenues. Within a couple years, however, the owner, Jack, ran into his own financial difficulties. In his desperation Jack sold the fruits of my and our coworkers' labor. I realized then that any business I didn't own myself would always be a revolving door. Jack's poor business planning and bad investments were also another lesson I learned by observation instead of the hard way: stick to what you know. Eventually, it also gave Sharon and me the opportunity to purchase two RTO stores in Alabama, one in Huntsville and the other in Muscle Shoals. I had only recently opened these stores as an employee of Jack just six months prior. It was the beginning of the second most important job I would ever have—business owner. The most important job was also coming to pass: becoming a dad.

Sharon: And Baby Makes Three

I loved the freedom Larry and I had at the beginning of our marriage. Our first home in St. Louis, Missouri, was the definition of a fixer-upper. It was a beautiful three-bedroom brick ranch with a private backyard, two-car garage, and a pool, but it was in sad shape. The previous owner was a young guy who housed friends as needed and hosted some wicked parties. Cleaning was not on his agenda, much less home improvement. At times they'd used the unfinished basement as a garbage dump, opening the door and heaving trash bags down the stairs. They left behind a full and moldy refrigerator and dishwasher, cabinets of food, dishes, trash, a waterbed, and the vermin that come with such poor cleaning habits.

The backyard pool was home to a multitude of frogs, mosquitos, and, we would discover, several pieces of lawn furniture. As it hadn't been kept up for some time, we couldn't tell what was concealed by the thick green muck that filled this "amenity" we'd just bought.

When we weren't building our careers, we were working on the house. I recall Larry emptying the in-ground pool one five-gallon bucket at a time, walking from ten feet deep to four feet and into the shallow end. Frogs, beer bottles, and mud were abundant on the bottom of the pool. We were so proud of that work. We became wallpapering pros and eventually turned it into a home, which became a gathering place for the people we loved.

I was so excited to have a dining room for dinners and holidays—neither of us had grown up with one, and it seemed like such a big deal to me at the time. We especially loved holidays with family there, and the pool became the hub for so many barbecues with friends and family. Larry was excited to grill corn and perfect his barbecue pork steaks for everyone. We even got a dog, Chelsea, who Larry's dad forever called Chauncy. She was an Aussie pup of Val's dog, Tess, with whom I'd fallen in love in those last months at U of I. Our lives were full and whole.

As much as I was certain I would get my degree before I ever married or had kids, I was just as ambivalent about whether I wanted to have kids. It wasn't exactly that I didn't want children, but it was more that I wasn't sure what kind of mother I would be and what it would be like having someone else so entirely dependent on me.

Yet, ambivalence can sway either direction, and at any given time I could entertain a future as a career woman without children and in the next moment could see myself raising a child. Ultimately, and with more than a little persuasion from Larry, ambivalence swung the baby way. Toward the end of 1983, Larry and I recognized how blessed we were and how much we had to give a child. I believed then that one child was doable without impacting either of our goals, and it was true.

I got pregnant easily, and Steven was born in November of 1984. My parents were at the hospital for his birth and were instantly in love. Steven wasn't their first grandbaby, but he was the closest in proximity. He had looming brown eyes and a cleft chin and was alert from his first hours. His grandma immediately began calling him her brown-eyed baby. We brought him home to his new nursery, and I marveled that love could feel so much more than I'd ever dreamed. My dad had made a cradle for him that sat next to our bed, and even in those sleepless nights early on, I kept thinking, he is perfect. Barb took off from work and came that first week to help with the newness. She was a hands-on aunt several times over by then and eager to help, though I most appreciated the companionship and comfort of her presence. Our neighbor cared for him after my six-week maternity leave was up, and I enrolled Steven in daycare once he was three months old. I returned to work, and aside from the weight gain, sleepless nights, and general tiredness, we were happy in our new routines and so excited to watch him grow and change every day. Everyone was thrilled to meet baby Steven, and he had more snuggles and sitters than any baby in history. When necessary I'd bring him to work to catch up on things, and he was adored there too. Home life was sweet, but work was wearing me down.

The bosses continued to demand different goals, and the hours were more difficult with a newborn. In care facility kitchens, the day starts at about five in the morning and ends at seven at night on a good day. It's shift work, and if a cook didn't show up for a shift, I'd need to find, or be, the replacement. I could see the job had limits and repeatedly requested to be considered for management training, even willing to go back to school or take a cut in pay while I learned. Everyone wanted me where I was, and my last salary increase reflected that I'd reached my limit in lots of ways. It was time to settle or move on.

I took what I'd learned in the jobs I'd held and at the nursing homes to apply and take a position with St. Charles County to manage the current jail kitchen and help design and build the kitchen and dining facilities at their new county jail. The old jail was built in the early twentieth century, and the basement cells resembled a dungeon. It had a tiny kitchen and an undersized storage room. Bringing the new jail into the future meant tapping into all my skills and passions to create a cutting-edge facility. The warden and county executives I interviewed with appreciated my two years of engineering and ability to think critically in terms of function. It was an invigorating opportunity for me. The possibilities seemed endless.

Larry was moving up quickly with Christa Rentals; I had rather easily gotten on at a new job making more money and with more opportunity. We had moved into our first home, bought a dog, and had a baby. Life together was great.

Life was perfect.

Larry: That's My Boy

On November 7, 1984, our lives changed forever. I remember that moment like it was yesterday. Sharon gave birth to our first child, a little boy, and he was so tiny and perfect. We named him Steven. I was afraid to break him. However, once he was in my arms, I never wanted to let him go. We had fulfilled a dream that early in our relationship I didn't know was possible. Sharon was not excited about us having kids in our early dating days, but here we were, years later, a family.

I remember the first time Sharon had to leave for an out-of-town trip and I had Steven alone for a night. I believe I fed him something wrong, and he had a huge blowout (if you're a parent, you know what I mean). There was crap *everywhere*. I tried holding my nose while rushing him and the poopy diaper to the shower, peeling my own clothes off as we went, because it was getting all over me too. Turning on the shower and holding him under it at arm's length was quite the challenge. Once again my amazement of what Sharon accomplished daily was quite astounding. Work, babies, and taking care of me was an eighty-hour workweek!

Your firstborn is so special, because their arrival changes you from identifying as someone's son, brother, husband, friend, boss, whatever, to being someone's dad. Becoming the person responsible for the security and comfort of another human being is a daunting honor. I wanted to give him everything I had at that moment, even if it was so little.

I had always been ambitious, but my passion for success meant something bigger once Steven was born. I knew I had to continue to be successful in my career. Four months after he was born was when Sharon and I bought those first two stores in Alabama in March of 1985. I knew to be successful I needed to control my own destiny, and when offered the opportunity to get out from under the seesaw of being someone else's employee, I knew we had to make the move.

I knew that as a young mother, Sharon had reservations, but together we ventured onward. We had little money, and negotiating the purchase was quite a challenge. The house we bought was underwater, as we owed more on it than when we bought it due to a scheme called adjustable mortgage, which had created negative amortization. Our assets were limited to a 1982 Volvo we had paid off and a few thousand in savings.

Early on I asked my dad if he'd loan me the $10,000 shortfall to begin my business journey. However, like when I left for California, he said, "You need to find your own way." So, we did. The financing company decided someone as motivated as me was a better financial bet than the original owner who had fallen far behind on the original loan. So, Sharon and I were granted a new loan of $192,000 from Transamerica with $20,000 down. After my dad said no, I had to get creative. So, we decided to refinance our car, and those proceeds, along with the $2,000 of savings and the sale of our house, which we had just spent over a year making a home that we absolutely loved, made us able to close the deal. Sharon and I were now the proud owners of two stores in Muscle Shoals and Huntsville, Alabama. Before Steven was five months old, we had loaded up the car and the U-Haul and began the trek to Alabama.

We were almost $200,000 in debt, living with our first baby in a crappy two-bedroom apartment with bugs and holes in the wall. We figured the only place to go was up, so we planned for grand success.

CHAPTER FIVE

The Business of a Partnership

> Love begins by taking care of the
> closest ones—the ones at home.
>
> —MOTHER TERESA

Sharon: Culture Shock

When you love someone as much as I love Larry, you never want to hold them back. It was easier to follow through with that support with the business because I always had faith in Larry and his business sense. Still, the move to Alabama was so much different from the time we spent in California, or living together back in Illinois, or even our eventual move to St. Louis. Actually, we had done so much moving, you'd think it'd be old hat at it by then, but Alabama threw me.

When we arrived in Muscle Shoals, we were back to apartment life, but with a baby. We had worked so hard on our St. Louis house, fixing it up and making it a home. We loved the location, the cozy den, and the big dining room for hosting family and friends. Though we had more than the tiny U-Haul we brought back from California, our belongings were no more at home in Alabama than I was.

The apartment was two stories with living room and kitchen down and two bedrooms and a bathroom up. Keeping Steven off the steps was a challenge, and I was plagued with images of him falling from the top of those stairs. The place was also dark, and there were roaches *again*! I battled them at my first job and in our first fixer-upper house, and I really thought I was done with roaches!

Sadly, we had little choice by the time we got there. Decisions had been made, and now it was time to get to it. I'd look for a job, I'd find a daycare, I'd make some friends, and everything would be great. Except there were no jobs and no daycares. The pace of life was impossibly slow in Alabama. Getting groceries or going to the post office was forever drawn out by an overly chatty clerk or a friendly shopper sharing thoughts on the buy of the day.

I stopped in a fabric store one night to grab something quickly, and the lady who was waiting on me began telling me about every dress she'd ever made for her daughter. I don't know why, but I just stood there and cried. The poor sweet lady took me over to a chair and was so concerned. That's how everyone was—chatty and kind. In retrospect I can appreciate the unique nature of the place, but as a young mother trying to adjust, the time required to do the most basic things wore on me early on.

One saving grace was that our move into a new house happened fairly quickly. Larry sold the Huntsville store in less than a year. It sold as soon as he could make a decent profit, paying down debt to the finance company and securing financing for the house. The store was an hour and a half from Muscle Shoals, and the time on the road was time wasted. We didn't even draw a salary for a few months when we moved to Alabama, so hiring upper management was out of the question. We did it all, worked together, and, with Larry's know-how, made both stores profitable in a very short time—and bought our second home!

The home was not just new to us; it was brand new. Our things came out of storage, the apartment was emptied, and we were home. The new home was a comfort, with a real kitchen, a large living room, three bedrooms, and a laundry/mud room easily accessible—and roach free! Bonus points because it was a ranch style, and everything was on the same floor—no more nightmares about Steven falling down the stairs.

I had given up the job of creating the new St. Charles County Jail, and there were no jobs available in Muscle Shoals. As an intellectually curious and hardworking person, I found myself helping Larry with his new business. I took over bookkeeping, payroll, and inventory. I helped in the Muscle Shoals store, working the front desk, taking calls, and making sales (the best I could). We didn't have software in 1985, so everything was manually tracked: payables, payroll, customer payments, deliveries, pickups—everything. It was tedious but simple, and it kept me busy.

Working with Larry was a new kind of education. He was so perceptive about the mechanics of business that it seemed intuitive with him to drive success. If you ask him, he can explain exactly what he sees, and I benefited from his observations. We all did. I was doing just about everything in the store at different times, but I quickly understood where some of the gaps were in our processes.

We had call cards for our clients that were to be used when they got behind on their weekly payments. The store was small enough that we knew the employees were calling the clients, but they forgot to keep track of when they called and the nature of the calls. This meant we could not rely on the information on the call cards. We might not be calling someone who had communication gaps, or we might be harassing someone who was committed to making payments. I'd already seen how poor communication in business could cause drama and problems, so I made sure to drive compliance with the stores.

As with management jobs in Alabama, the daycare centers were few and far between. Instead of a formal daycare, Steven stayed with a woman in her home a few days a week while I helped at the Muscle Shoals store. I had also taken a part-time job at a craft store, and one of the ladies there recommended this sitter. One day I went to get Steven, but no one answered my knock. I walked in the front door, and there were three babies sitting in a semicircle of highchairs unattended, some crying, and some eating Cheerios and what looked like yellow cheese.

I didn't see Steven, so I rushed down the hall to find him in a playpen in the back bedroom, just staring up at me. The sitter "had just stepped out" to get something from a backyard shed. I was fuming. We never went back.

Steven ended up joining the family business, and he often accompanied me in the back office where I did books, and the store became like a surrogate family. He was so cute toddling around the store, climbing on sofas and pushing TV knobs willy-nilly, but one day a furniture dolly fell on him and bruised his spine. It was a frightening encounter, and thankfully it wasn't serious. We were doing what we could to make it work as a family, but it wasn't working that great. So I was surprised to learn within a couple months of our move to Alabama that I would be having a second baby before Steven's second birthday.

Larry: Patience and Opportunity

We arrived in Alabama with $192,000 in debt, when in my entire working career I doubt if I had made much more than $200,000 total. How would I pay it back? My dad was a firm believer in pay it back quick and avoid that interest. I was motivated to make the two stores work.

During the four years I worked for Jack, we'd opened and sold close to a hundred stores, so I knew I could manage two. When Sharon and I started our own stores, the Muscle Shoals store was doing a whopping $12,000 in revenue a month. The new Huntsville store had just opened and showed revenues of $7,000 my first month. I signed a note for ten times that monthly revenue, which was how the $192,000 was calculated.

Splitting time between two stores was not my dream; it required more time, not less. We had a new baby and another on the way, so being gone more was unlikely to make for a happy marriage. Still, as a business owner, I understood I needed to work extremely hard to make a profit. I did that, and we grew the business quickly.

The concept of rent to own was new and basically relied on a handshake. The clients needed no credit, and we did not rely on a credit score to allow them to rent from us. Instead, we asked for their signature and a few local references to secure the transaction. It still works the same way to this day. Just return the product, or make payments for twelve to eighteen months to own it, or pay it off early. The concept was simple, and it was based on need. Our clients needed a way to get clean clothes, keep cold milk, and enjoy entertainment for ten to fifteen dollars per week. Revenues grew quickly, because clients pay people they like, and I never let them down. The business was built on relationships first, ahead of transactions.

I believed in marketing our business, and I spent a great deal on TV commercials in the market. Sharon created our first script, and our local TV stations made Rent One a standout in the marketplace. Within less than a year, we were noticed by a regional rent-to-own company. This recognition made it possible to sell our Huntsville store and reduce the debt from the original $192,000 to just $60,000 on the Muscle Shoals store.

Aside from the debt relief, selling the store also eliminated my daily commute. Now, I was all in on the Muscle Shoals store. I could work less and make more. The finance company, Transamerica, was ecstatic with the stability, the new owners got a solid deal, and the Carrico family was going to start enjoying life in Alabama. That was what my brother Keith calls a "*Win, win, win!*"

Unlike when we lived in Illinois and had parallel careers, in Alabama Sharon was indispensable in our business. Her diligence in our accounting procedures contributed to our success. I knew our audits and inventory were reliable under her leadership, and that allowed us to make informed decisions about what needed work and where opportunities existed. I had the utmost trust in her partnership.

Many businesses fail because one partner is creating but no one is completing compliance activities. This was never an issue with Sharon and me. Sharon could do everything in the store, even sell a TV. However, selling was not Sharon's cup of tea.

Sharon: Sweet Home Alabama

Alabama summers are hot, even in northern Alabama. You'd think being pregnant would have been miserable in that heat, but I barely felt pregnant most days and don't even remember the heat. I can't recall where I went for prenatal care or my doctor's name. I can't find any pictures of me when I was pregnant with our daughter and barely remember anything special about those nine months. I don't know why—maybe it was the move, or the new business, or the second baby news—but I gained only twenty pounds. My body was so unfazed by the pregnancy that when I walked into the hospital in labor and told the nurse I was having a baby, she looked me up and down and said, "Girl, you're not even pregnant." But I was definitely pregnant, and Nichole Marie was born on September 9, 1986, in Florence, Alabama.

While the pregnancy left no impression on my memory, it ended with a memorable birthing story. An incredible nurse held my hand and talked me through every pain and push. I had an epidural with Steven, but that mercy was not available in this hospital. The next best thing was my angel nurse.

The Eliza Coffee Memorial Hospital was also under renovations at the time, and some genius had decided to move maternity to the old children's ward. It seemed fine, and even cheery, in those primary-colored walls—until I had to use the toilet, which was toddler height and required painful acrobatics to get on and off the seat postpartum.

My parents came down to Alabama and spent a week helping us settle in at home. Through those months in Alabama, I had the feeling that we were doing it—that we would make it. I was always optimistic about finding my way, getting a job, or going back to school. The babies didn't deter anything; maybe there were delays, but they did not deter.

Then Nicki developed an ear infection that spread to her blood when she was about six weeks old. At first I took her daily for anti-biotic shots, but she eventually ended up hospitalized so she could receive an IV antibiotic. Then she got pneumonia. She stayed there a little more than a week, and it was numbing and frightening and left me feeling fragile. By the time Nicki was home, being a mom to my two babies under two was what mattered most to me. Doing the books for the store only took a few hours a week, and I gave up my part-time gig painting for the craft store. I was home most days, and the time flew.

I can't tell you how I spent my days aside from snuggling babies, cooking, and doing bookwork. I do remember thinking that Steven was so serious as an infant and toddler—it took a lot to get him to laugh—and I decidedly wanted to be more jovial around Nicki, thinking it would set her up for levity. I've since learned that kids are born with these temperaments to some extent, and on any given day Steven will out-laugh Nicki to prove the point. Aside from that, I also spent a lot of time cleaning up the red clay dust that seemed to take over the house daily. We had put sod in the front yard and plugged the back but didn't hang around long enough for it to fill in, so the windows stayed shut and the red dust persisted, and we were very well snuggled and content and jovial in these little routines.

Larry: Millions of Reasons

Living in Alabama had its own challenges, and when Nicki became extremely sick, I knew being closer to family would be a huge advantage. It's hard to look back on the timing now and not see God's hand in it, but as my daughter was gaining back her strength, I got a call from Transamerica. Because I'd so quickly reduced my initial debt to them, from $190,000 to $60,000, they wanted me to buy six more failing stores in Southern Illinois. When the opportunity to return closer to home was presented, I knew we had to take advantage of this opportunity and get back to our family support group.

The opportunities continued to grow over the next few years. I chose wisely when I knew I could turn a store around or grow a new one, and so did the creditors. I routinely borrowed and repaid faster than most in the industry, which was ultimately rewarded with traditional bank financing.

When we first moved to Mount Vernon, Illinois, and began our business relationship with Boatmen's Bank, they required me to place a $10,000 CD on deposit before they would allow me to open a checking account for my store accounts. I had never been required to do this in the past and was puzzled and pushed back but to no avail. I assumed the bank's relationship with the previous owners was less than stellar, so I accepted the medicine, knowing I would prove them wrong.

Eventually, we developed a great business relationship, and they purchased my debt from Transamerica. This arrangement made Sharon and me one of the first RTO dealers to secure traditional bank financing. Eventually, I would be appointed to a community-level board of directors. In 1988 with prime at 10 percent, plus the 5 percent additional risk charge, it was a huge amount to pay.

My dependability and track record meant that I asked for concessions, and most were granted because I always paid my debts first, even if I did not get paid. I was investing in my reputation, and it provided dividends in opportunities.

That original note from Transamerica was almost completely repaid in less than a year, eliminating significant risk and leaving them in a far better position with us than they were with the previous owners—my old boss and his son. Jack, my previous employer, had split his company between him and his son, and their struggles to grow the business were evident. The son, Steve, decided to get out of the RTO business completely and called me in Alabama soon after we moved. He shared his revenue numbers with Sharon and me, hoping to sell us his newly acquired side of the business.

We reviewed Steve's numbers closely. Upon further review his situation was not what he presented, and we declined to purchase his six stores in southern Illinois. However, within a couple weeks of Steve's approach, Transamerica offered to sell the same stores directly to us, after they were to foreclose on Steve. The mortgage holder's price was substantially less than what Steve asked. So, my line of credit was extended to over $1 million to purchase and grow the business.

Aside from the business risk of our first million-dollar deal, we had the family to consider. Selling the home in Alabama meant giving up a home we built from the ground up. Moving back into a tiny two-bedroom apartment was quite the challenge, especially with two babies and now another on the way.

The year was 1987, and this was a big decision for us as a young couple. Still, we would be moving closer to home. So many people had faith in our abilities, and we knew it would work well. I remember thinking, "They believe in us, or they would not loan us the money to create success." I didn't personally meet Zig Ziglar until the late '80s when Sharon and I went to his trainer seminar for a week, but I'd been a fan of his long before, and Zig was a firm believer in "You will get all you want in life, if you help enough other people get what they want." This was what we wanted to achieve.

Zig also said failure is an event, not a person, and I truly believe one needs failure to obtain success. I can write another book on failure, but one cannot dwell on past disappointments. I don't believe we ever thought we would see success at our current level or that we would be bankrupt either. We were always cautious with others' money and knew they believed in us. It was never in my character to let them down.

Sharon and I were loading up the U-Haul again and going back home to Illinois, now with seven stores and two kids.

CHAPTER SIX

Homeward Bound

> Do ordinary things with extraordinary love.
>
> —MOTHER TERESA

Larry: Boomtown

Moving back to Illinois was exciting, but we had to be strategic about where we lived. We wanted to be close enough to our parents that they could spend time with the two grandchildren we already gave them and the third on the way. We also didn't want to be so close that we couldn't focus on our business or our own growing family.

We had to choose a new home location, not just for the soon-to-be five of us but also for reasonable access to our seven stores—the original one in Muscle Shoals and six new Illinois locations. Looking at the map and considering the distance I would need to drive between locations, the confluence of interstate highways 57 and 64 and several state highways meant that Mount Vernon would be the best location for our new headquarters and our new home.

We were about ninety miles away from family, closer than when we were in Alabama but far enough to begin a new life in a new town. We were also just a highway trek away from our stores in Carbondale, Centralia, Harrisburg, Marion, and Cairo. This geographic decision would be fortuitous for us as we grew our business and our family in the years to come, but we needed to start somewhere, and that somewhere was Mount Vernon.

Our first corporate offices—because with seven stores we were a corporation now—were headquartered in the back warehouse of a storefront. It got ridiculously cold in there during the winter months, but the business was heating up.

Sharon: Hometown

We moved into a two-bedroom apartment when we arrived because we didn't have time to house hunt before taking on the new stores, and we had to sell the house in Alabama. I like to believe that I'm not spoiled or needy, but put me in an apartment with small children and it's obvious I'm both. Most of our things were in storage, and the lack of space, the stark white walls, the closet laundry (that wasn't grounded and shocked me with every load), and the rowdy, crowded, loud, and looming neighbors are memories that agitate me to this day.

Once we started house hunting, driving the streets of Mount Vernon with a realtor, I got the feeling it was a small town on an expansive plain and it was all at once too open and too closed off. Main Street with its central county courthouse was the biggest draw, but it wasn't much. It was tired, and I was immediately hopeful we would not be here long.

Until we found a better solution, I relied on a local girl to babysit Steven and Nicki while I helped at the Mount Vernon store. It was

1987, and inventory tracking was being done on a computer system—manually entering new inventory from Larry's paper purchase orders. Every delivery, pickup, charge-off, payout, and weekly mailing of receipts from each store needed to be recorded. Once in Mount Vernon, we adapted the previous owners' accounting software, and I began processing payroll and payables electronically too.

I had taken computer science and data entry courses in college, and it was helpful to understand the logic in those early days of DOS operating systems. Our software supplier, Cass Systems, was a lifeline to me for many years as we expanded and integrated operations. Time was fleeting and marked by weekly, monthly, quarterly, and annual routines—bank reconciliations, inventory audits, depreciation runs, payroll, financials, taxes, and W2s became the rhythm of my life. This million-dollar debt was ours together as much as our kids were ours together, and I was determined to help us succeed at business and at raising our family.

Once we sold the Alabama house and it was time to leave the apartment, instead of moving into town, we chose to live in the country early on. Our house was on three acres, up a small hill outside of town on Tolle Road, where we had some privacy and some contact with nature. The neighbor's horses would frequent our side fence line for treats from the kids, the woods across the street provided their first mini-adventures, and the expansive field behind the house blessed us with incredible sunrises. I loved the house and yard and even the woodstove that had to be kept burning to warm us through winter months. Maybe I was just glad to be out of the apartment, but I have wonderful memories from Tolle Road and all the firsts we experienced there.

One of those firsts was welcoming our third baby! I found out I was pregnant when we were still in Alabama, in Spring 1987. I cried. And, sorry Kelly, they were not tears of joy. It seemed we had just gotten settled. Steven was only two but potty-trained; Nicki, at six months, was healthy and sleeping through the night. We were in a cute little house, with a picket fence around a beautiful back yard, and I remember being excited to start looking for a swing set. Then Larry came with news of more stores in Illinois, which meant another move, and then the pregnancy test came with a plus sign.

But by December 10 of the same year, we were elated to bring Kelly home to that house on a hill in the country! She has been my constant reminder in life that God's plans are greater than our own—we cannot see what He sees or know what He knows of our futures. I hate that I was not happy when I found out I was pregnant and that I was so afraid. But then Kelly was here to turn it all around to joy! I was barely checked in to the hospital when she decided it was time to be seen and heard—before the doctor could even get in his scrubs! She has been setting her own agenda ever since, and I marvel every day at the ways she makes our family complete.

Larry: Small Town

Not long after we first moved into our Tolle Road home, nature beckoned Steven. I was cutting the grass, and Sharon's parents were there helping us burn our moving boxes. With adults occupied outside with chores, Steven toddled off. After a frantic search, I found him trapped in a field near our neighbor's house. Steven was caught in a bramble, his overalls wrapped up in the branches and pinned by the briar thorns. Steven was angry as a hornet for being trapped. I supposed he saw himself as stuck, not lost, but I was relieved to find our three-year-old and get him back to the house.

Mount Vernon was going to be a place where the kids, when they were a bit older, would be able to roam and experience small-town life. One of the best parts of success in Mount Vernon was the ability to give back to the community that supported our family and our family business. We sponsored local teams, even as our kids were part of those leagues, and provided uniforms.

The kids' time in sports brought back fond memories of when my mom and dad were still together, making popcorn and mowing the ball field of my own youth. Now, I was the dad, and it felt good to see my own children reveling in that wholesome community. They started with T-ball when they were small, but as they grew the kids all played soccer and basketball through the YMCA.

During the week I was working but still part of the community. I served as president of Kiwanis in Mount Vernon. Sharon was able to get away for lunches at the Elks club to support their mission while promoting our business and making connections. As our involvement grew, so did our profiles, and we became recognized. Being on television didn't help with our family's privacy.

Within five years we had fourteen stores. That growth was good business strategy aided by strong marketing. By 1989 we had become so ingrained in the community and successful in the business that the bank was willing to finance our inventory.

At the time no one in the industry had banks willing to finance their inventory. Instead, my competitors were paying higher interest and higher premiums for their inventory. In the 1980s most of the industry was at the mercy of Transamerica for financing trust receipts of our inventories. They facilitated a third-party financing that was five points over the prime interest rate, which meant rates as high as 21 percent before any sales were made, and the industry was losing hundreds of thousands of dollars in interest. We were losing the same way on those rates, until we were able to use more traditional financing through an established bank. That was a game changer that gave us a strong competitive advantage for growth through acquisition of other stores that were failing under less favorable terms.

Rent One set itself apart by espousing the same values the Carrico family held for hard work and paying our creditors on time and in full according to our contracts. Our consistency meant we were given better deals, and the more we grew, the better the deals became. We treated our creditors and our vendors the same way we wanted our customers to treat us. Of course, that didn't always work in our favor with our customers in every deal, but it set a pattern. We built a solid reputation and trust both in business and in the community.

Sharon: Small Town

As we settled into our life in Mount Vernon, we gradually, and by the providence of God, returned to the Church. Steven had been baptized by Father Kuhl in the same church where we were married, while we were still living in St. Louis. We drove up from Alabama to see Father Kuhl one last time for Nicki's baptism in 1986. Kelly would be baptized at St. Mary's in Mount Vernon by Father Vandelou. While these rituals were initially to appease my mom, I started to feel a familiar stirring that God was calling.

The kids were all attending a daycare run by Logan Street Baptist Church. It was more than a daycare; it was the support and guidance my kids needed, and I needed it too. I will forever be grateful for the staff and the administrator, Jeanne, who loved us through all those years. If you are a young mother, please work hard to find a support system that does more than keep your kids safe. It is only now that I understand and appreciate all God gave me when Jeanne and Logan Street entered our lives.

I soon found myself at the local Christian bookstore searching out cassette tapes of kids' Christian music to listen to on the drive to and from town. I picked up some great reads and my own tapes of Steven Curtis Chapman, Amy Grant, and Michael W. Smith that I would later purchase on DVD and, again, on iTunes years later. Whether it was the Catholic church of Larry's and my childhoods or the community of the Logan Street Baptist Church and their warm and open pastor, we felt the warmth of community raising our kids among a fellowship. As in those youth group meetings and college Bible study days, I once again felt God carrying us along every step.

Logan Street Baptist offered us the beautiful foundation of a loving preschool for all three of our children. From 1987 when we first moved to Mount Vernon until Kelly finished in 1991, we had a child at Logan Street. As a working mom helping Larry build our business, I was thankful for a genuine safehold for our small children where I never had to worry about finding them unattended or disengaged.

The children went on to Catholic school for elementary, just as Larry and I had done. By the time all three kids were in school, it made sense for us to move closer to town so we had less driving and easier access to their sports and our social obligations with the business. So, we built a new house in 1991. We'd been married eight years, and we had moved nine times. This time the house was built for a family of five and meant to last us many years.

Our years in Mount Vernon were marked by service. It was wonderful that we could sponsor teams and be involved in fundraising through the Elks and Kiwanis, but we wanted the kids to be part of the giving. We wanted them to grow up with a giving spirit, and Mount Vernon made that possible. All three kids, now in their thirties, fondly remember the days spent volunteering with Meals on Wheels and serving stacks at Kiwanis pancake breakfasts. Being closer to town as the children grew older made service more accessible as part of our whole family ethic and lifestyle.

Larry was on practically every board and in every club possible. He frequently traveled to check up on the stores, and I wasn't sure if he was genuinely giving back, drumming up business, or avoiding the chaos of home, but he was busy! I had joined a group called Mount Vernon Newcomers and got on as treasurer of the St. Mary's school board, where I made it my mission to build a decent playground for the school. Its completion is one of the things I'm most proud of in our years there.

My parents had also become regulars in our lives, usually traveling with us on vacations every year and coming to see us almost weekly. Mom would catch up the laundry and have dinner ready when I got home from work whenever they visited. I kept a running list of repairs and fixer-uppers for Dad. They still had their place at the lake, so we drove to Litchfield a few times every summer to spend weekends camping and boating with them. We were in a good place for a time, but as the kids got older, the rhythm of the work schedule, the sameness of the streets, and the tediousness of daily life seemed to settle on my spirit.

CHAPTER SEVEN

Feeling the Heat

> If you go looking for a friend, you're going
> to find they're scarce. If you go out to be a
> friend, you'll find them everywhere.
>
> —ZIG ZIGLAR

Larry: Authentic Growth

Our family involvement in the Mount Vernon community grew along with the kids. I had never been involved as a volunteer in any organized group prior to our move to Mount Vernon, and when asked to speak about my business at a Kiwanis business leadership meeting, I was skeptical.

Why would they ask a thirty-year-old guy just starting in business who rented out TVs and furniture to speak in front of established businessmen who had the world by the tail? Before this meeting I was forced to pay extreme interest rates to borrow money, had to place a

$10,000 CD in a bank to open an account, was criticized by consumer groups for charging too much, and was attacked by politicians until they wanted a donation for their campaign.

I learned a great lesson from these Kiwanians, and it changed my view on life. You must ask to receive, and the rewards I received from this great community organization changed my perspective on life. They didn't want anything, just my involvement. From that day forward, I felt honored that my help was needed and my opinion was cherished.

Once I became a member of the Kiwanis, I served in many capacities over the ten-plus years of involvement and even served as the president. I served on the board of the Jefferson County Chamber of Commerce and the economic development board and loved to coach for the YMCA and St. Mary's athletics.

A game changer for our communities and coworkers in southern Illinois was our financial match program through the United Way. Every dollar a coworker donated through a payroll deduction program was matched by Sharon and me through Rent One. Eventually, this led to us forming our foundation, Great Expectations, which allowed an additional match from Sharon and me personally, so every dollar an employee donated ended up as three dollars to a charity. The more involved Sharon and I became as individuals, the clearer it became to me that the company could do more for our employees within their own communities.

We implemented a community giving program at work and sponsored our employees' memberships in civic organizations like the Kiwanis, Lions, and Elks clubs. Aside from building visibility and credibility in the communities where we did business, investing in our people meant those connections were meaningful. Anyone can buy a commercial, but not everyone puts their sweat equity behind a community, and that's what we were doing as individuals, as a family, and by supporting our own employees. In this way our influence in giving could be greater by establishing a sense of stewardship in the people we hired and, in turn, improving the very communities where we owned businesses.

This mentality was not reserved for community involvement. Sharon and I both attended a Zig Ziglar Train the Trainer weeklong session in Dallas. This opportunity to work with Zig and his team had a profound influence on how we would approach our internal training and development of our managers over the coming decades.

We also committed to Dale Carnegie's fourteen-week program and then brought our managers in for the same life-changing education. By developing the skills and mindset from the top down, I was able to support more growth for our leaders and other leaders in our larger community. I served as a mentor and as a teaching aid at official Dale Carnegie events. We learn more when we teach and practice the principles. Enriching my own understanding and experience helped me be a more stable influence on the employees and the community. It was a beautiful cycle that was ever expanding to encompass others, who then spread the principles of ethical success to those they led. Carnegie's *How to Win Friends and Influence People* was a simple solution; however, it needed to be genuine and sincere. Once understood, it changed the person and made a difference in their family's livelihood. At one time over 75 percent of our leadership team had graduated from this life-changing course.

Sharon: Crossroads

When we decided to move closer to town, we chose to build our new home. The process of building another new house from the ground up was exciting, but it was also hectic. The planning and making of decisions ate tons of time from an already busy schedule but was so worth it when we were finally inside our new place. It just took some time.

We planned on moving in early 1991. The builder's wife, Dorothy, was our real estate agent and suggested we put our Tolle Road home on the market in summer of 1990. We were afraid the distance from town would make it a difficult sell, since that's why we were selling it. Our concerns were valid, and we had few lookers and no offers until November.

Once the price was settled, the buyers demanded a thirty-day close date. We asked for an extension, explaining how we really wanted to be in our home with three children for Christmas. However, they wanted the same thing. They wanted to be in their *new* home for Christmas with their kids too.

Because it took so long to sell, we capitulated. We had no home for Christmas, old or new. We packed up everything, put it in storage, and, luckily, Dorothy found us a short-term rental where we made do for a few months. I remember how I didn't even want to decorate for Christmas, but the kids kept asking about a tree. Finally, we had the delivery guys bring a tree from our Mount Vernon location that was part of the store's holiday decorations. It was a crazy time and getting crazier by the year.

We had grown the business to fourteen stores by then, and I could barely keep up. I hired Lori, the girl who lived down the street on Tolle Road (our one-time babysitter), to help with inventory and another lady, MaryAnn, to help with payables. Systems were improving, but I still had tons of data entry and verifications to get done each week. I was traveling to stores a lot to install, upgrade, and maintain computer systems and still doing everything else in the office up to annual taxes. It felt like I was on autopilot.

Larry and I disagreed on some key management decisions, and, remembering my own headaches with a husband/wife owner, I decided to stay out of the stores' operations. It was enough to manage the corporate office while taking care of everything at home.

In the fall of 1993, we were busy with school, and sports, and music lessons, and Scouts, and all the things. Steven was starting third grade at St. Mary's, with Nicki in first and Kelly in kindergarten. We were struggling, or really I was struggling, with the school and the principal, Sister Helen. She was an old-school disciplinarian who didn't hesitate to frighten the kids into good behavior. At one point Steven was acting up at lunch, and she grabbed him by the ear and hauled him out, quite aggressively by all accounts. I played with the idea of sending him to public school, and even his teacher felt it was worth a try.

I went to one parent-teacher conference and noticed a chart tracking math progress; only Steven and maybe two other children even knew all their multiplication tables. This was a goal set by the teacher the previous month. I asked her if they were moving on to division, and she said they couldn't until everyone was caught up. So, she just kept going over multiplication. It was frustrating that three kids, including mine, were being held back by the performance of the class and the school. I set up a learning center upstairs for the kids and bought into the book series What Your X Grader Needs to Know, because it seemed like they were all capable of more than what St. Mary's was offering.

The following year Steven slipped off a picnic table at recess and was taken to the local hospital. He lost consciousness after he hit his forehead on the concrete. His nose was also bloodied by the fall. The hospital took X-rays and released him, saying he was not seriously hurt. A few hours after we were home, he was dizzy and vomiting. I took him back to the hospital, and they transferred him to St. Louis. He fractured his sinuses, had a concussion, and would spend a week in the hospital.

I had seen Nicki hospitalized as an infant and again when she broke her leg at age three. We'd made numerous trips to the pediatric orthopedist in St. Louis for that injury. We'd made semiannual trips to have Steven's heart checked every year since we moved to Mount Vernon when his new pediatrician found a murmur.

I'd been to the same St. Louis hospital with Kelly just three years earlier when she swallowed a nickel and it got stuck in her esophagus. The Mount Vernon hospital was not sure how to treat her, and after over seven long hours in the ER with the surgeon and anesthesiologist bickering, I picked her up and drove her to St. Louis myself. It was a routine procedure, and she'd have been released immediately after if the nickel hadn't been in there for so long. We ended up staying two days for observation. I was growing weary of the kids' school, weary of the healthcare available to my family, and weary of my job.

Our social life, to the contrary, was booming. We'd made countless friends through St. Mary's, various civic organizations, and a new membership at the Elks club. We partied every weekend, worked bingo at the church every month, and attended social and civic events at every opportunity. I loved our friends and the freedom of those nights without balancing numbers or kids.

By 1994 we were up to fifteen stores with no end in sight. We had been through a horrific audit the previous year, where the state of Illinois was claiming back taxes and penalties due that would put us out of business. I had called and verified when we filed for our state tax number that we should be collecting sales tax and not use tax for the rental transactions. Now the state was saying the opposite.

The auditor was, excuse my language, a complete ass. He said I'd need to have that in writing to abate the balance due. I dug up the files for Illinois sales tax from 1987, and the notes from my conversation were on the front. He told me he didn't care and said I should have gotten it in writing. I will never forget the guilt of that oversight, but then what did I know in 1987 at twenty-eight years old and a new business owner about how government works? The previous owners were collecting and remitting sales tax, so I followed suit and verified by phone.

We worked so hard and had given up so much in those eight years, and we'd come so far. Now it looked like we'd done it all for nothing. We ended up in court and with another long wait to learn our destiny, and we eventually won the case. But the threat and the waiting had added many straws to the rhetorical camel's back. They were tucked in there with the straws of mother, daughter, wife, and employee.

Larry expected a strong partner, a classic and ideal family, and my support in whatever he deemed worthy of his attention. With twenty-one stores, there was a lot worthy of my attention. We had recently remodeled our offices and brought in Larry's brother, Keith, to take over my HR duties. I had help from Lori and MaryAnn, but the tide of work never seemed to ebb. We hired a bookkeeper, Donna, and kept plugging away. Somehow, I never saw the big picture; I just kept doing what needed to be done day to day. It didn't seem like we were growing toward anything except more churn. We had more revenue but no security. A customer had sued for falling in one of our location's entryways, and an employee was claiming an on-the-job injury with life-altering disability. I didn't want anything more than what I had by this point, so it all seemed like a futile game, except I knew it was working, because Larry believed in it so strongly. So, I kept showing up.

My dad had cancer that was completely removed by surgery, but the fear of losing him hit us all hard. It was difficult having our kids question why their papa was so sick, seeing them at his bedside, and contemplating a world without him in it for all of us. He had always been so strong, and now he wasn't. My mother had spiraled in her OCD over the past few years too. Her boss and some new technology were frustrating her at work. Her hands were blistered from checking doorknobs, and it was taking her longer and longer to even leave her house. She called me several times a day to check in and talk. I didn't have time or patience for her, and I felt numb toward her agony. It seemed like a problem she could solve if she put her mind to it and sought help, but she didn't, and I resented her for staying in that mental state for so many years. I had no idea then how hard it is to fix some things but would learn in time.

I had started taking lunches at the Elks, first with friends, then just by myself. The food was good, and the beer was cold. I began to linger longer than the lunch hour, and sometimes I didn't go back to work at all. Larry would call, and I'd tell him to get the kids Burger King, that I'd be home when I was ready.

I lived for those weekend nights out and weeknight social gatherings. I joined a lady's golf league (having never golfed before), but I enjoyed the drinks and shots more than the game every Thursday after work. For the longest time, the beer and bars meant time shared with Larry and friends, and laughter and comfort. It was an escape from too many demands, but, gradually, it made me stop caring about those demands—the taxes, the bank reconciliations, my mom, what was for dinner, and even the kids.

Those fun weekend nights would end, more and more often, with me sobbing on the closet floor, depressed, and wanting out of my life. I even left town a few times. I'd get in the car and just drive away to anywhere. I ended up in St. Louis once, in front of our first house where we'd brought Steven home from the hospital. I wondered how different things would have been if we'd been able to stay there. I wondered what career I might have, what friends, and opportunities I never experienced because my life went in a different direction. I wanted out, but I didn't even know what I wanted out of, much less how to get where I needed to be or where that was, exactly.

I started counseling at some point and vaguely recall those sessions. Maybe I didn't start soon enough, or maybe it wasn't the right person, but it didn't help. By February 1995 Larry had decided to "fix" the problem. One day he just said we were going to visit the store in Centralia and go to lunch. We drove to St. Mary's Hospital in Centralia where he had arranged for me to be admitted to their drug and alcohol rehab program. He was clear that if I didn't go, I would not be going home either. He implied that the kids would not be going wherever I was going, and he would eventually fight for custody. I was so confused. I loved him but hated him. He did so much for me and for us all but expected so much too. We were partners, but it felt like it wasn't fifty-fifty anymore. I was not in control of my own life. I went to rehab.

Sharon: Fresh Starts

When I got out of rehab in 1995, everything was different. We had hired a bookkeeper, Donna, and she'd taken over everything in just three short weeks. I worked a while, but being back in the office made me feel small somehow. I didn't belong. I wasn't convinced that drinking was the problem, but I promised Larry and myself that I'd give sobriety a year and evaluate. I couldn't imagine my life without drinking, but I had to try.

After Donna was comfortable, I thought I would try being a stay-at-home mom. Staying at home meant staying away from the Elks club and the golf course and even social gatherings for a while. It turns out I hadn't socialized much without a drink in my hand since high school.

I went to ninety meetings in ninety days, then twice a week. I was hanging out with new friends from rehab and meetings; old friends were not calling anyway. New sobriety is so hard, and while I was on antidepressants, it would take almost two years for me to get my head in a better place. I had friends from rehab who, at the time, seemed like family. They got me through days and hours of crazy thinking and jitters and cravings. They were welcomed in our home and came and went frequently. Over the first year, some returned to their addiction, some lasted in recovery, some died. Larry went to Al-Anon, and the kids even went to Alateen for a bit but hated it. I was nowhere near sane, as evidenced by the remnants of a tattoo I got to celebrate my six months of sobriety. It sounds crazy now, but the smallest thing would go wrong, and my immediate thought was, "I wish I were dead." My sponsor suggested I put a rubber band on my wrist so I could snap it every time the thought arose, so I'd change the thought, intentionally, to one of gratitude. It was an old AA trick, used when you think you want a drink, but it began to work on my depression too. It was a shock to me when I realized one day that the thought of killing myself hadn't popped up in over a week. I was lost but slowly started putting one foot in front of the other. All the meetings and therapy were working (at a snail's pace it seemed to me), but I quickly realized I was bored. Luckily, our church needed a bookkeeper, and since I was experienced, I began working in the parish office.

A neighbor who knew I was struggling suggested I start walking regularly, and so I did. I also took some classes at the local junior college. I planned to get my degree in education—if the schools weren't good, I'd change them from the inside. I read books on education, unionization, and the politics and policies of academia. I planned to transfer into Southern Illinois University at Carbondale to get my degree. I was making a comeback and would find a new dream.

Then the fire happened. It was likely faulty wiring sparked in the basement of our Mount Vernon store and corporate office's location. Everything was gone overnight, and I felt called to help. Early on the burned-out building offered almost nothing salvageable. I thought, before I saw how violent and impossible the fire was, that I might get in the back to retrieve *something*, but that was not to be. The fireproof safe would eventually be found beneath a literal ton of bricks, but it was fireproof, not heat proof, and its contents were damaged. We did go back days later, and one of us grabbed a brick from the aftermath, and that brick is still in our possession to this day.

After the fire the corporate offices set up shop in a car dealership. I knew the processes and wanted to help. We had lost everything, and even the computer backups were compromised. We'd developed a system for off-site storage, switching disks regularly with one set in a fireproof safe at the office and another in a safety deposit box. The on-site files were ruined, and somehow the off-site files were corrupt. Since our office was in the back of a store, that store's customer files and computer information about those customers was all lost.

I felt responsible. I'd helped implement the process for backup, and it had failed. Again, we were in crisis. I had to help, but when I showed up, I was told there wasn't anything I could contribute. I hadn't worked in the office regularly in almost a year. I went back to the church office and my coursework.

It was time to head to Carbondale and get enrolled. I drove the sixty miles south and talked to a counselor. My transcripts and application had cleared, but the courses for a degree would be a full-time job or a lifetime endeavor if spread out. I drove home debating my options. I couldn't take many courses with a family and an hour-plus commute one way. Online learning was a thing of the future. It seemed like I was out of options, but then a new opportunity emerged.

Rick Linton was a creative marketer who had moved into a back room of our Marion, Illinois, Rent One store, but he was struggling with the business operations of his company, Imagery Marketing. I took up a position helping him get things in order, traveling to Marion three days a week to work in the office. This evolved into a partnership when Larry bought into Imagery financially to keep it afloat. I was soon there five days a week.

I was now working in my own business, wholly separate from Rent One and outside of Mount Vernon. This new opportunity fed my curiosity, and I dove into marketing books and the emerging internet boom. I was able to use my operational skills to help ensure the success of Imagery while finding ways to be creative in my role.

The rent-to-own business never had a great reputation, and the industry's marketing approach bordered on tacky. Imagery Marketing was the key to branding Rent One as the standard-bearer for quality marketing. We pushed the image of our business in a direction that gave it a degree of dignity that was novel and satisfying. David Ballowe, hired as a graphic designer, would eventually become our creative director and was key in all things branding and in the agency's success along the way. Imagery Marketing introduced customized printed materials, looping in-store video, and online shopping to the RTO industry. While doing the work for Rent One, we were able to package those programs and resell them to other RTO businesses outside of our territories.

We grew the company from a head count of four-and-a-half employees to twenty-six in the years that I was in leadership at Imagery Marketing. Rick Linton became an invaluable mentor and partner on this journey. Marty Smith, a Rent One employee, was transferred to Imagery to head up sales, bringing in and retaining long-term customers in the rent-to-own space. We also brought in software developers before marketing companies had IT departments so we could exploit the emerging technologies, just as we had done when we digitized Rent One's back office and inventory systems. Those innovations at Imagery Marketing jumped to Rent One, and we collaborated on industry best practices that were adopted across the RTO space.

It was challenging, and I didn't like a lot of what leading a marketing company entailed, but I loved other parts of the business. We had the absolute best team assembled. Every single person contributed something essential. We all worked together and celebrated together and commiserated together, and most of all, we laughed together. We were building a company together, and everyone played a part. I hope each employee that worked with me there really knows the gratitude I feel for their time and their gifts shared. I miss those days.

Larry: World on Fire

With fifteen stores and growing still, we took the first major challenge to our business. The Illinois Department of Revenue (DOR) approached us to review our records and spent close to a year reviewing every purchase and tax filing we had completed. He was combative, where we were cooperative. Finally, the day before we were scheduled to leave on a well-earned and much-anticipated family vacation, we were served with his audit results. Hearing those results I remember making some derogatory comments and offered him and the state the keys to our store.

We had a $230,000 tax debt due to a conflict between sales and use taxes. We were told the clock was ticking and interest was accruing at 1.5 percent monthly, and I needed to accept the amount or face additional fines and interest. Sharon and I had taken great pains to be compliant on every front, and as ethical people we knew we didn't intentionally avoid taxes, so we fought back, and ultimately, after two long years of court battles and numerous nights without sleep, we won in the state appellate court. We were able to successfully show that the state had received a windfall and we didn't owe any additional tax. It was a complicated process; however, as passionate business owners, we were able to show we were correct.

With all the issues from the audit impacting our business, I grew to understand I needed to be involved with local, state, and federal politics. I began a journey to involve myself with our national trade association, the Association of Progressive Rental Organizations (APRO). We immediately organized the Illinois Rental Dealers Association, of which I served as president. We met with legislators to make sure laws protected not only Rent One, but the other three hundred–plus RTO locations to eventually be opened throughout the state of Illinois. Our national trade association was key to the beginning stages of this still-new transaction that required no credit and allowed consumers to return the goods at any time.

Emboldened by what I was learning, Rent One continued to develop grassroots efforts on all levels of state and federal politics. I started to be involved in our state and national associations and developed skills that explained our transaction to the political leaders of our state and federal government. Never would I allow others to define our rent-to-own transaction without my two cents. I invited politicians to our stores, introduced them to our coworkers and clients, and showed our involvement in our communities in Illinois. Sharon and I were able to put a face on a transaction that allowed people to have the nice things they needed and wanted. Cold milk, clean clothes, entertainment, and a great night's sleep are essential for everyone, and the pride of ownership was only twelve to eighteen months away. Our clients and coworkers grew up together, and even today I recognize many of the Mount Vernon clients from 1987.

It's been a joy to see their kids and grandkids return to do business with us. Many of our clients have succeeded in managing their money to obtain traditional financing, or many now save and purchase items outright. The laws our dealers and I helped develop over the years provided transparency and disclosures that helped all our clients to obtain ownership in a variety of ways. For every product we rent to own, we disclose weekly and monthly amounts with total price to own, a cash price to purchase today or in ninety days, and whether the product is new or preowned. These simple rules/disclosures have created a win in forty-seven states. In the early days of the 1980s and 1990s, we were attacked by many consumer groups; however, RTO dealers around the country won them over with grassroots efforts by welcoming legislators into our stores to show our wares.

The next business blow we took was much more damaging to our livelihood but also taught us even better life lessons that helped expand our business in ways we never would have imagined before it happened. Looking back it seems unlikely that we would have come out of the disaster stronger, but we did.

In April 1996, nearly nine years after moving to Mount Vernon, we had twenty-two stores, but we were about to lose one to the fire. Our home phone rang in the middle of that spring evening. As Sharon and I drove out of our subdivision and turned toward the main part of downtown Mount Vernon, the sky above the little town was aglow from the raging blaze. It was too hot, dangerous, and loud for anyone who wasn't part of the fire department to even consider approaching the street, much less the building. The word conflagration was invented for just such a fire.

Our Mount Vernon store was absolutely destroyed along with an entire block of buildings. We lost inventory and property, and that loss was compounded by learning we were underinsured. We also lost fourteen years of information that I kept in my ledgers, because our corporate offices were in that building. Gone were over one thousand active rental agreements and all the associated client information. Our tape backups were destroyed along with all our business books.

But the goodwill we built up in the community began to pay off. While roughly 25 percent of those renters disappeared with the opportunity to keep their property without paying for it because the contracts and proof were gone with the fire, another 75 percent did pay us back. Ironically, many of those people were those who had fallen behind at some point, because we found them through tracking slips we used to call past-due clients. These documents survived in a small ten-by-twenty-foot storage building in the southeast part of the building. The wind had blown from that corner, and the fire had expanded northwest. Those paper documents allowed us to track and rebuild the $1 million in potential lost revenues. Those tiny pieces of paper were grouped together on portable tables in the back of a car dealership service bay. As Zig always shared, adversity multiplies the end benefit. Lessons learned the hard way are very memorable.

We learned we needed to have a different approach to our business after the fire, and we bought our first building. The five-acre site would be the nucleus of our new twenty-thousand-square-foot, state-of-the-art Rent One location. The site came with a twenty-thousand-square-foot Ace Hardware store, and we added another twenty-seven thousand square feet to house new tenants to help pay for our new site by renting to other merchants. If the fire had never happened, we would never have been forced to consider buying instead of renting.

The adversity of that one terrible disaster became an opportunity for us to build a real estate business. Over the coming years, that new property would include over one hundred stores and occupy over one million square feet of commercial property, of which we own five hundred thousand square feet. With the mix of larger and smaller stores, we own close to 40 percent of our business fronts, and we lease real estate to other businesses. The roots of that success were planted in the ashes of a fire that taught us how to handle adversity as opportunity.

Of course, along the way, I was cautious and only purchased real estate in communities where we had a successful Rent One and knew it was a viable investment. Our business model is to operate in small communities versus larger cities. We believe community is important, and we can make a greater difference in smaller communities. At a Rent One store, every coworker knows your name.

We continue to implement advanced technologies in our stores. From our humble beginnings when collaborating with Sharon's Imagery Marketing, we grew our own IT department well before our competitors considered such a thing. We leveraged SharePoint when it was a brand-new technology to preserve the information we had to rebuild after the Mount Vernon fire. All my black ledgers with ten years of business revenues were lost in the disaster; however, that lesson served as a catalyst for growth not only in a physical sense but also in technology. Our leadership now understands that we are sometimes better off allowing other great companies to support us to avoid the mistakes we made in the past and we can rely on their entrepreneurial acumen to help us achieve greater success. We learned many great lessons and are better prepared for the future because of our difficult discoveries in the past.

CHAPTER EIGHT

Experiments in Beginning Again

> My wish for you is that you continue.
> Continue to be who you are, to astonish a
> mean world with your acts of kindness.
>
> —MAYA ANGELOU

Sharon: When It's Time to Go

In 1996 we moved Imagery to Mount Vernon and switched the kids from St. Mary's to public school. It was an easier decision than I expected it to be. The public school's curriculum was good, and the extracurriculars were exceptional. Socially, it was a smooth transition for the kids, as all three kids knew most of their classmates. Many of the kids at their new schools were neighbors from our own subdivision. School was now within walking or biking distance for the kids.

I was working hard on sobriety and taking tiny steps to be more social without a beer in my hand. I was on antidepressants and attended two meetings a week for the next four years. I continued therapy and worked the AA program one step at a time, one day at a time. There were days, even hours, when I thought it was impossible to hold on to sobriety, but I'd call someone in the program, or go for a walk, and that day, that moment, would pass. A year after my sober date, things had already begun to change. In AA we tell our story under the premise of what it was like, what happened, and what it is like now. My story in a nutshell is like this:

> *I used to drink for fun. I drank to be social. I didn't have to drink to get through a day or a week, so I couldn't be an alcoholic. But by the time I got to rehab, I was drinking to avoid my life; I tolerated my life. It felt like I had no choices, and no matter what I wanted, it didn't matter. When I got to rehab, I was depressed but didn't think drinking was the problem at all. If you lived in this small town, with my controlling husband, my tedious job, a mother who needed care herself, and three small kids to keep up with, you'd drink too! Life had just happened, one move and one kid at a time, without a lot of input from me. At one year sober, I was already beginning to see that with the same husband, the same mother, the same kids, and the same small town, I could find moments of happiness. I had choices, like whether to drink or not, whether to take Mom's phone call or not, whether to work or not. It might have been the drinking after all—wink, wink.*

I was growing in sobriety, but my faith had taken a hit. I wasn't sure what to believe anymore, and now it mattered more than before. It was hard to go to church; it was even hard to recite the Our Father at the end of meetings. I'd switched out the words "give us this day our daily bread" to "give us this day our daily strength." I tried Logan Street Baptist Church again, and I ceaselessly prayed the Serenity Prayer.

God must have heard, because the kids had to enroll in the parish school of religion (PSR) since they were now in public school. There was a need for teachers, so I signed up and taught seventh and eighth graders all about the significance of the Mass, the lives of the saints, and the basics of covenant theology. As often happens when we teach, I learned more than they did about my Catholic faith and bought my first Bible study guide.

By Spring 1997 I quit my bookkeeping job in the parish office and was full time at the growing Imagery Marketing. Steven was finishing seventh grade, Nicki in fifth, and Kelly in fourth. The public school was set up with a sixth-grade center and a junior high separate from the grade school. The transition brought a lot of students together from different parts of town.

We had some trouble with Steven in sixth and seventh grades. Most parents I discussed it with said it was typical, but for me it seemed like an omen of what high school would bring when even more kids would merge from county schools. My gut told me, even though he was a phenomenal athlete and student, that he would not do well at Mount Vernon High. He was choosing the wrong friends and making bad choices outside of sports and school. I started looking at our options.

Mater Dei Catholic High School was fifty miles away in Breese, Illinois. I couldn't imagine that commute for school or extracurriculars. Larry and I discussed sending him to boarding school. Chaminade College Prep in St. Louis seemed like the best fit, and we investigated it and even discussed getting an apartment or condo in St. Louis so we could stay over easily and visit more often.

Still, we didn't like the idea of having Steven out of our daily lives so young and soon realized we might be faced with similar choices for the girls in the coming years. We could be empty nesters way before our time! That's when the idea to move *again* came to us.

Imagery was growing, and we had brought in our sales pro, Marty Smith, who was traveling around the country selling marketing to other regional RTO dealers. We had lost our top design talent because he wanted to be in a bigger city with more opportunity. It seemed like moving the business, and the kids, would solve a lot of issues. And so we did it!

Larry: Ready, Set, Go

We lived in Mount Vernon for twelve years, building up our business from our first handful of stores to twenty-two stores in 1996 and twenty-eight stores just three years later in 1999. As the century turned, we were running two businesses, Rent One and Imagery Marketing. Sharon had developed Imagery to a respected business in the rent-to-own market space and began to find outside clients in the banking industry as well. Rent One had grown to include five corporate employees and over 150 employees across the twenty-eight stores.

I was heavily engaged with APRO and serving at the national level with a board position. I was learning how important regulation and advocacy were for any industry and would be able to use that knowledge in the months and years to come. For the time being, I was ready to move the family to St. Louis, Missouri, but my business was still in Illinois. Specifically, Rent One was staying in Mount Vernon for the time being.

Sharon: Begin Again

Though the well-being of the kids was a primary reason for our move to St. Louis, it was not an easy move for them or us. Mount Vernon was a small town where everyone knew everyone. St. Louis is sprawling by comparison. City limits are small, but most people live in the suburbs, and they go on forever.

The commute alone made our days longer. I had hoped to put the girls in our local church's parish school to finish grade school but encountered a wait list for both their grades. I wasn't sure it was the best option anyway, because we discovered that they would only be there a couple years before having to change schools, yet again, for high school. We looked for and applied to private schools that went K through twelve. After the interviews and applications and tours, all three were accepted at Mary Institute and Country Day School, and Steven also got in at Chaminade. He decided on the latter, and the girls would attend MICDS. We moved the summer of 1999.

All three kids got busy quickly with school, sports, music, friends, and more. We took them back to Mount Vernon frequently. Nicki struggled more than anyone, leaving a tight group of friends there. However, she stayed close with them through high school, even going to the Mount Vernon prom her senior year.

I commuted three days a week until we could move Imagery the following spring. Larry was the hero, commuting five days a week until he set up an office at Imagery and cut it down to less. Sometimes it is hard to believe he even agreed to the move, he was so rooted in Mount Vernon and invested in so many ways to making it better. The commute was anything but easy, one-and-a-half hours each way, and he did it for years. But he did agree, and just like that we had moved yet again, and this time it felt like coming home.

Larry: Experiments

Though we would be living in St. Louis, the Rent One corporate office was still in Mount Vernon. It took me until 2009 to feel comfortable moving Rent One's corporate office to Missouri. Until then I drove ninety minutes each way three days a week. Two days a week, I worked out of Sharon's Imagery offices in St. Louis for several years. After almost thirteen years of commuting and sharing offices at Imagery and Convergence, I decided to purchase a building large enough to house Imagery's crew, which had grown to over twenty people, and our small accounting office for Rent One. Much of our leadership for Rent One was dispersed around the four states where we did business.

In the time between the family move and the Rent One move to Missouri, I tried my hand at a variety of businesses. One of those was an internet service provider (ISP) providing dial-up to customers in southern Illinois. I would buy lines of dial-up service and resell to our customers on a weekly payment schedule. Like many of my experiments, it began with my desire to self-serve a utility or service that I felt was overpriced in the marketplace. Internet service for the stores and the corporate office was necessary, but it was an expense layered upon the expense of an extra phone line at that time in the late 1990s and early 2000s. An investment in an existing company called Convergence Communication, with a new partner, Rob, was my approach to taking control of the ISP and long-distance bill. We began to resell services to other businesses. However, AT&T and Verizon had a corner on the market and eventually caused our demise.

I also launched a brand-new wireless internet service called Poof Wireless in Carbondale, Illinois, and provided point-to-point internet services to student housing and many of my local Rent One stores and clients. I was able to provide higher speeds than traditional dial-up by installing bundled DSL cable at my local store in Carbondale. Then service was dispersed around the community with point-to-point devices. I looked like a hero, buying the bulk service and selling individual lines to clients for less than I was being charged, until Verizon. So, the big boys won again. I tried to bundle basic phone service, dial-up internet service, pagers, and long-distance service. I wanted to control the means of production for the utilities I was consuming as the owner of Rent One. Success was sweet while it lasted. However, as is always the case, failure was an event, not a person, and we slowly had to wind down all these services over time.

My work with APRO made me more highly aware of regulatory issues, and that prepared me to venture into these services. This experience with services, and the partnership with Rob at Convergence, then prepared me to develop E-sponder following the September 11 terror attacks in 2001. The concept behind E-sponder was to enable first responders in each state that we served to better communicate and track communications when responding to incidents. We were able to push text, email, and phone connectivity to all first-round responders within minutes. Our communication boards showed who had been notified and their response. In 2001 this was advanced technology few considered.

E-sponder was successful, but success brought challenges when the governor of the state of Missouri threatened to sue us for hiring away its first Homeland Security director. We avoided a lawsuit, but they did cancel our contract with the state of Missouri. Other challenges we faced with E-sponder included being paid by state and city municipalities that only had annual budgets. Every year our agreement needed to be renewed, which caused a renegotiation period that many times lasted until the following renewal. We were never paid on time and often had to threaten cities with terminating services. Cash flow was extremely poor and caused many sleepless nights. Other software and tech firms began to compete, and ultimately it was better for us to sell E-sponder to a competitor.

E-sponder, Convergence Communication, and Poof Wireless were great ideas at the right time but required a lot of time and resources. Early on we were able to sell the service to college campuses and other retailers. However, keeping up with the different industries as they grew and changed so rapidly required much attention to the details. While not impossible it would have taken even more of my attention away from Rent One and our growing real estate interests.

Other business ventures during the early years in St. Louis included owning some Radio Shack franchises, integrated into the Rent One store spaces. It seemed like a win to operate a franchise and discount costs on essentials needed for the stores, but when I got into the books, I realized I could buy inventory more cost-effectively through the Rent One wholesale market than through the franchise agreements. I got out of that at the right time.

Eventually, I turned my full attention back to Rent One. Aligned with the RTO business, we added Reliable Audio and Video and a jewelry rental option at select locations. At one point I tried car stereo rental and installation with some of our stores. In the same automotive vein, Rent and Roll was launched in 2006, where we have success-fully offered wheels and tires (or a safe way to work) to our clients with eleven locations in four states with over seventy-five coworkers. Eventually, the wheel business slowed, and the franchise changed the branding and name to RNR Tire Express, and success has been substantial. Results for some of these experiments were mixed. However, one client need was indisputable—a good night's sleep.

We have more recently launched Passport Sleep in our RTO portfolio. While mattress manufacturers are seeing shrinkage from competition from online providers, Passport Sleep is doing substantial business. Just like cold milk and clean clothes, everyone needs a great night's sleep, and mattresses are something people who don't have credit or ready cash are willing to pay for on terms of a twelve-month, same-as-cash program. People need a great night's sleep to perform well at work, and waking refreshed is so important for one's attitude because it does determine one's altitude. By focusing on the core mission of fulfilling a need for our clients, we continue to grow.

Later, with my focus still on Rent One operations, we opened a resale store that was New to You, with returned and refurbished Rent One merchandise we sold for cash. We had an inventory of preowned products at extreme discounts. College students and many just starting in life found this attractive. Adjacent to the resell store in the same building, we had a service center to repair TVs, appliances, and furniture that failed to work at Rent One. The greatest advantage of the rent-to-own business is all repairs are covered while people are making payments on their products, so there is never a repair bill. We would provide the client with a working washer, repair the one in their home, and return when service was completed. We eventually closed the resale shop and focused on repairing the clients' products very quickly. We later expanded into a forty-thousand-square-foot facility to repair products in eight states.

As change is inevitable, we needed to close our service center in 2021 and sold our forty-thousand-square-foot facility and jobbed out our client services to those who are more efficient. Like so many other business ventures, when times change we must find greater efficiencies. Our best-designed efforts must be critiqued to achieve success for all. We continue to be very cost conscious, and our leadership team provides valuable and insightful advice for us to make profitable decisions for our clients, coworkers, and communities. We have learned to watch the bottom line, but we know we can't know everything. The one infallible truth, as business grows, shrinks, and changes, is that failure is an event—not a person.

CHAPTER NINE

Family Business

> Life is like riding a bicycle. To keep your
> balance, you must keep moving.
>
> —ALBERT EINSTEIN

Sharon: Rough, Tough Stuff

We settled in St. Louis as a family, and everyone adjusted to their new environments. Imagery would move from Mount Vernon to St. Louis in the summer of 2000, making things much easier for all of us. We rented an office space near our new home and worked with an interior design firm to make the space both functional and beautiful.

Most of the staff made the move with us, including our partner Rick Linton, two designers, and a videographer. I called our best creative, David Ballowe, who had left Mount Vernon for Chicago a year earlier, and convinced him to come back. I remember taking him on a tour of the new offices before we even moved in. We had a beautiful reception area, conference room, workstations for six designers, two video web stations, a video editing suite, a print and assemble area, a sound booth for recording, and plenty of offices for support staff.

I told him that when we filled the place up, we'd be finished growing; midsize was big enough. He was excited to be part of the vision and came on board. Together, we filled up that office space and then ended up having to move two more times over the years as the agency expanded.

Our lives were expanding in other ways too, as the kids' lives became bigger with their new social circles and activities. The girls were thriving. The size of their school, the pace of their day, the friendship drama of middle school, and new social norms to learn kept them engaged and busy. Both were active in sports and taking music lessons, and Nicki found a new passion for theater and art that would shape her adult life.

The school required participation in a sport each semester, and Nicki tried them all! We saw her skills at high jump, soccer, field hockey, basketball, even yoga and rock climbing. She eventually found her place in cross country running and would be cocaptain of the team her senior year. Kelly's competitive nature found relief in club sports and camps. She would become a star field hockey goalie, a sport we never even heard of before moving, but it is huge in St. Louis.

Aside from friends and school and sports, we were on a social bender. We had class parties, parent parties, recitals, games, awards ceremonies, and, new to us, bar and bat mitzvahs, sweet sixteens, and social etiquette clubs like Fort Nightly, Junior League, and the Veiled Prophet Ball, a coming-out event that none of us appreciated in theory but took part in out of intrigue and what would later be known as FOMO (fear of missing out).

Steven started out strong at Chaminade and found his place in wrestling, baseball, and football. He was a naturally gifted athlete and a fan favorite for his passion as much as his skill. He was forging ahead his freshman year with academics and athletics; it seemed the move was good for all of us.

Toward the end of his freshman year, however, things took a turn. Steven had a fallout with his group of friends, and it didn't get resolved by the time school started back in the fall. He wouldn't talk about it, so we just kind of watched him stumble along, hoping things would get back to normal. Instead, he found a new group of friends and began making similar bad choices to what we'd left in Mount Vernon.

By the end of his sophomore year, our own experience convinced us that drugs and/or alcohol were a big part of the problem and sent him to outpatient rehab. It didn't help, and things escalated quickly; by midsummer, we felt out of control. We talked about military school and researched inpatient rehab facilities. We settled on an outdoor wilderness therapy and rehab program in Bend, Oregon. He spent a month there, wandering the mountains, learning to start fires with a crossbow, discovering the pain in long pack hikes and in self-discovery. He came home to start his junior year, full of hope and promises, but broke them, and our hearts, and our family by Christmas of that year.

It was 2001, and the girls were settling into the newness of St. Louis. For their sake and ours, we told most people their brother was at camp, which was not a total lie. I didn't have many close friends in St. Louis yet and didn't trust the new ones with the truth. Having a child battle addiction was, and probably still is, wholly isolating. I pulled back from friendships that were barely budding. As a family we did less and less socially to avoid questions from people who might hear rumors or have the scoop from their kids.

Steven was expelled from Chaminade and enrolled in the public high school for the second semester of his junior year. He would be expelled from there too and finish high school with a homeschool diploma the following year. I remember cringing when the phone rang back then, hating to answer it for fear it was the police or worse. He was in fights and car accidents. He had numerous arrests. He was not my son as I had known him, and still I felt his pain more keenly than my own. I wanted to heal him, but I could not bear his burdens for him.

Outside our home we pretended to be normal and continued to show up at all the games and parties and ceremonies for the girls. We appeared like everyone else, happy and whole, but we were hurting for our boy and being hurt by his turmoil.

Work had grown more and more demanding over these years. Engagement with the business probably kept me from going completely insane. It was something to focus on and pass those days in some routine and purpose. I guess it made me feel useful and productive—in retrospect, it was a lot like the band playing on the deck of the *Titanic* as she took on water. What else is one to do? As I said earlier, most of the time in life we all carry the good and the bad together. There are sweet moments on the worst of days; there is sadness in the best of times. We get on with life, give thanks for the blessings, and ask God to help us carry the burdens.

Larry: Contractions

I enjoyed sampling the business opportunities available in the earliest part of the twenty-first century during those first years we lived in St. Louis. I like to say that failure is an event, not a person, and I had an ebb and flow of failures and successes, but nothing I tried was ever as successful as the RTO business.

Dialing back my experiments in business, I was able to redouble my focus and my efforts on Rent One and our real estate portfolio. In 1999 we understood 80 percent of our critical business issues were in big city markets like St. Louis. Our best leadership members were from small towns in southern Illinois. Their integrity and work ethic were unquestionable. Rich Bergman was an original hire in 1987 who I found under a van changing a transmission when I arrived to work after taking over the company. His dad was a coal miner, and my dad was a union man at GM on the line—both had never missed a day of work. Rich and I had the same work ethic. What he and I lacked in book smarts we made up for in outworking the rest. I stressed before that your attitude determines your altitude. Rich moved and ran so many stores I can't recall them all. He was able to go from changing a transmission for seventy-five dollars to running forty-four stores in several states. To this day his work ethic is beyond question, and he now runs our RNR Tire Express franchise in eleven markets.

Understanding the losses in smaller markets were 20 percent of the bigger markets, we began to swap big-market stores for smaller areas. Our first acquisition was to exit six stores in the metro St. Louis area for four stores in southeast Missouri. Those four stores became the base and understanding for additional small markets. The industry was beginning to consolidate. The larger players in the industry were not able to exist in lower revenue areas; however, our model began to flourish. We were able to go from twenty-four stores in the late '90s to forty-four stores eight years later in 2006. Revenue had more than doubled. We were growing our team and establishing some great talent.

We understood the need to expand leadership if we were to continue to grow. We began to create VP positions and regional managers to grow the operation. We overstaffed leadership and always chose leaders by work ethic and desire to succeed. Trent Agin, who is now our president, had followed a similar path as Rich by going anywhere that was needed. He worked next door at the IGA grocery store in Harrisburg, Illinois, when our first employee, Elvis Riley, recognized his desire to succeed.

Trent's vision for developing talent was a key to his success. His humble beginnings in the late '80s to leading a team of six hundred coworkers and one hundred–plus stores in eight states are extremely admirable. Over the last thirty-five years, I have purchased, sold, traded, and opened over two hundred stores. Within the last twenty years, Trent was always wide-eyed and attentively listening to every detail to create a win for both the RTO dealer who was selling or buying stores and the teams of coworkers. He has gained honor and extreme integrity over his years of leadership in the industry; Sharon and I appreciate his leadership.

So many additional members of Rent One have allowed us success. We knew HR was a key to any great company. I was able to lure my brother, Captain Keith Carrico from the US Air Force, in the early 1990s to help run our HR department. Once again work ethic, balance, and absolute integrity were at the top of his game, as he created our training department using insights and efficiencies he learned in the air force. He has created an open-door policy that all understand. You can always talk to Keith.

Lori McGovern, who began as our sitter for the kids when we moved to Mount Vernon in 1987, is now our VP of Information Services. She is self-made. Her respect in the industry and in our company for our software systems is unmatched. If you need to know it, she understands it and will share it or fix it. Again, she's another core member of our team.

These coworkers were the original team in the first couple years; however, they were able to find great talent to create additional wins, and many others have now helped us create success.

Along the way we understood the image of the industry was a challenge. We decided to control the branding and cost by buying many of the buildings or shopping centers we were having success in. I understood the value of real estate would stabilize our balance sheet, and why not pay myself as well?

I was placing improvements in my buildings, not another landlord. Several things began to be clear: our coworkers loved the new look and enjoyed coming to a nice store, they saw their revenues grow because our clients liked the look and layout, and the value of the buildings could be leveraged to buy more rental products to grow. As my brother says, it's a *win, win, win.*

We saw over the years many reasons to purchase and occupy our buildings—none better than when we were able to turn an unpolished stone into a diamond. We now own over 40 percent of our locations. Many of our new builds include Rent One and RNR in the same center with a few smaller shops in the middle that help offset the cost of ownership.

Going back to what worked, we continued to grow our portfolio. We held steady at fifteen stores until 1996 when we grew by nearly 50 percent to twenty-two stores. We opened seven more stores again the following year, doubling our footprint to thirty-one stores in just two years.

The growth sometimes reversed by a store or two over the ensuing years, as we consolidated stores or closed in markets that were not drawing the right employees who could beat the competition.

However, growth was steady overall. By 2009 we had fifty stores, and by 2016 we had seventy-six. In 2021 our team was running 114 stores.

Kelly and Steven are the next generation of leadership who are already contributing in major ways to our success. Like Rich, Trent, Lori, and Keith, the emerging leaders in our corporate family are leading from within to bring us success throughout.

Sharon: Expansions

When I was shivering on the porch bedroom of Valerie's house trying to earn my way through college and finish my degree, I promised myself that if I ever had kids, they would not have to work so hard or make choices between eating or a bus ride. I wanted it to be a full experience for them, where learning was their only responsibility and joy was at hand if they chose to reach out and take it.

The girls took all the college trips to scope out the best fit. Each applied to multiple schools, and both ended up at their first choice. Their work in high school and the amazing curriculum, staff, and emphasis on whole-person education had paid dividends for both girls. While they were reluctant to move from Mount Vernon, both are so very grateful today that we did.

That said, it's always important to point out that many kids from Mount Vernon and its surrounding rural communities have found tremendous success and joy in life. As a parent I simply saw that I needed a different environment for myself to best raise my kids. I needed more structure and support for them and a team to help me be the kind of mom I wanted to be. For so many reasons, I felt unable to steer them on my own toward the life I dreamed of for them without the extra support we could get in St. Louis.

Steven's path to higher and continuing education was not a straight line, but he did make efforts and attended classes at local colleges in the years after high school, including Maryville University, University of Missouri at Saint Louis, and St. Louis University. He eventually reached his bottom and surrendered to sobriety in November 2007, when he found himself without support or enablement from us, his friends, or a long line of girlfriends. It is for another time, another book, to tell what all took place in those years and how we all carried the burdens and blessings of that time. I will simply say I am still rejoicing that he became one of the miracle stories of AA. So many stories of people who struggle with addiction do not have this outcome. This seems like the perfect place to plug Alcoholics Anonymous and Narcotics Anonymous. It is free, and it works—if you work it. And you're never late to your first meeting! It astounds me today, after twenty-six years of my own sobriety, that the AA promises are still coming true.

The AA Promises

1. If we are painstaking about this phase of our development, we will be amazed before we are halfway through.

2. We are going to know a new freedom and a new happiness.

3. We will not regret the past nor wish to shut the door on it.

4. We will comprehend the word serenity and we will know peace.

5. No matter how far down the scale we have gone, we will see how our experience can benefit others.

6. That feeling of uselessness and self-pity will disappear.

7. We will lose interest in selfish things and gain interest in our fellows.

8. Self-seeking will slip away.

9. Our whole attitude and outlook upon life will change.

10. Fear of people and of economic insecurity will leave us.

11. We will intuitively know how to handle situations which used to baffle us.

12. We will suddenly realize that God is doing for us what we could not do for ourselves.

Are these extravagant promises? We think not. They are being fulfilled among us—sometimes quickly, sometimes slowly. They will always materialize if we work for them.[1]

Even though she grew up in a small town for her most formative years, Nicki always wanted to go to a big city. She only looked at schools in major urban areas and fell in love with New York City. It was no surprise she headed to NYU after high school, eventually transferring into its prestigious Gallatin School of Individualized Study. There she designed her own curriculum that she had to present and have approved by the board. Nicki was a dedicated student, graduating a semester early with a degree in storytelling and visual media. She found her calling in documentary film production. While at NYU, just as she had done in Mount Vernon, and just like she had done in St. Louis, and just as she is doing today, Nicki continued to make lifelong connections along the way.

---

1   W., Bill. 2002. *Alcoholics Anonymous: The Story of How Many Thousands of Men and Women Have Recovered from Alcoholism.* New York: Alcoholics Anonymous World Services.

I admire her constancy and dedication to her goals. Her steadfast pursuit of what she wants to accomplish and her ability to accomplish it while taking care of herself and surrounding herself with a loving chosen family far from home are impressive. She is a strong woman in her own right, but she also gets homesick, which is fine with us because we miss her and love to have her home as often as she can come.

Kelly's approach was, interestingly, more experimental than designing her own education. She wanted at first to be a marine biologist and ended up at the University of Miami in Florida, which was a major party school. Kelly, having experienced family members with addiction, was always the designated driver, never a party girl. She was the child who, in high school, spent a considerable amount of time at home on the couch and always called for a pickup at midnight if things got out of hand. So, when she went to Miami, she didn't fit exactly. She made the best of it and, a girl who loves to dance, went to all the night clubs, often as the designated driver. She made it three semesters before spending her fourth with Semester at Sea, a program that took her on an amazing and life-changing journey. After that trip she had a clearer vision, and realizing Miami was not the life for her, she changed majors and schools and came home to St. Louis. Kelly finished her degree in business with a focus on leadership and change management at St. Louis University and began her career near family.

While the kids were pursuing their educations, whether at major universities or the school of hard knocks, I was figuring out what was next for me, not knowing just yet that it would also be back at college.

Larry: Family Business

The struggles of our family life over the last forty-plus years have built the culture of our family and business. I hope to continue with both for as long as possible. Has it been easy? I can recall the many calls from Sharon while I was on the road; they brought tears to my eyes in those days, and I struggled to know why I was not present. But her strength, tone, encouragement, and gentle manner inspired me to continue. I had to ask myself if I was staying out on the road because I was afraid of the battles at home or to create success for many.

As we continued to pursue ownership of select Rent One stores instead of renting our storefronts, the business was reaching a tipping point. Steven was coming into his own in his residential real estate career. We were struggling with lease renewals and the ability to manage the tenants who came along with some of the centers we had purchased. I needed someone who was a trusted advisor, so who better to pose the opportunity to than Steven? We offered him the position, and he shifted to the commercial side of real estate. It was a great pairing for him and LDC Properties, the property trust for our owned properties, to become the director of real estate for our business.

Though Steven has a gift for negotiation and contracts and is a natural wordsmith, he certainly didn't start out as a director. Rather, he started at our tires and wheels business making ten dollars an hour and commissions. He worked in the wheel and tire business and took the necessary courses to get his real estate license before taking a leadership position in the property side. I remember many times where he would meet with the tenant and review their business model and share how a dollar or two a client could help the bottom line, allow them to gain additional success, and sometimes pay more rent! Seldom does he miss an opportunity to visit with our long-term tenants. Yes, they appreciate the concern he shows.

Like Steven, Kelly took a circuitous route before joining me in leadership at Rent One. Kelly, also like Steven, worked at an entry level early on. She spent the first two years after college supporting the business without a title. While doing that she met a motivational speaker we were using, and he lured her away to partner with one of his businesses in Utah. She was already an entrepreneur, and she learned failure early. It was an event, not a person. Eventually, she came home and tried again with a CrossFit business. I was proud of her for trying, just like I had tried, and when the business eventually failed, Kelly the person dusted herself off and began to immerse herself in the regional position at Rent One.

Kelly's drive and need for success were evident, and she was extremely successful running a region of eight stores. She did so well that she ended up running four regions, and at least thirty stores were under her in that role. She was voted employee of the year by her peers. I had no vote, but I was so proud to see her thriving at Rent One. Now Kelly is the VP of Strategy and Culture, a much-needed position to grow our business. When she began the position in 2018, we never realized how important it would be during the pandemic.

I'm always trying to lure Nicki back home to help us *grow* the business. Her creativity and work ethic are second to none. My conversations with her are like how mine and my dad's were. *Why do you not get paid for every hour you work, Nicki? Oh, Dad, I am moving them along.* I am so proud the next day when she comes back and tells me that she got what we discussed. Nicki is humble but dazzles employers with her level of success. There are few people who have her genuine level of concern for getting it correct every time.

10

Faith in the Future

> True music must repeat the thought and
> inspirations of the people and the time.
>
> —GEORGE GERSHWIN

Sharon: A Time to Every Purpose

As the kids grew into their adult selves, I dove back into work at Imagery. We had moved twice to accommodate growing needs like larger video and web departments. We had added a media buyer and copywriter and a project manager. Larry moved an accountant in from Rent One to manage the financials and bookkeeping staff. He also placed his brother in charge of our web department. We were churning dollars with slim margins, and I felt he wanted tighter management to improve profits.

We had several large St. Louis–area clients and enjoyed significant success in online shopping/payment systems early on in this technology. We had developed in-store video programming for our RTO clients and were working hard on an education platform to train Rent One and, hopefully, other clients' employees.

I was busier than ever, and the demands seemed endless. Clients wanted results, products, and frequent changes. Their wants required so many meetings and so much time. Employees wanted more benefits, more pay, and more feedback. Their wants required even more meetings and more time from me. I was working fifty to sixty hours a week, more now than ever in my life. With cell phones and emails and online access, I was taking the work home a lot of nights. One day I found myself wondering why I was working so hard at something I never dreamed of doing and was liking less and less. Within a month I'd made the decision to retire and move on.

In retrospect it sounds like an easy decision. It was anything but easy. I'd put sweat, tears, love, and so much time into building a company where people actually *wanted* to work. It was a place where we toiled and triumphed in unison. We were solid and growing still, but it was crushing me in a lot of ways.

The bigger the clients, the bigger the projects, the higher the revenue, the higher the demands. Larry's involvement was a factor too. He envisioned bigger margins, tighter management, larger clients. We had consolidated Rent One and Imagery offices at one location, and he was in on meetings and major decisions. I had uncomfortable memories of working daily with him in Rent One. I was always heard and appreciated, but I was not equal. It may have been my own weakness or misperception of reality, but I knew I could not work with him that way again. I recall meeting with my partners and two top staff before making any decision and explaining my fatigue and my perspective on Larry's involvement. I asked for their help and stressed that if things stayed on course, it felt like I'd have to choose between my marriage and Imagery—I could not work with or for Larry again.

In hindsight I should have gone to Larry and told him to step away. However, if you gain anything from this book, it should be the understanding that he is a force unto himself. When there is a goal (particularly financial or business oriented), he is unstoppable. When I was in college, it felt like I was his goal. For a long time, success and the family were his goals. At the time I decided to retire, it seemed Imagery was in his sights. I had other avenues for fulfilling my needs. It was exhausting to me to even think about opposing him, and I was growing weary of the hours and struggles. So, I decided to quit, began looking for a partner to take on my role, and backed away over a year's time.

Before I even retired, I knew I wanted to go back to school. I'd taken courses on and off over the years and have always loved being in the classroom. It is mind-blowing to me the amount of knowledge in the world we have never touched, the depths of research, history, intellectual curiosity that have gone before and continue. I love it all! My focus for my first degree was science heavy, so I chose to pursue a degree in English. It was an opportunity to build on my understanding and practice of liberal arts and creative work after my time in marketing.

I was always an avid reader, yet a void in my comprehension of all the nuance of classics meant CliffsNotes had been my best friends in my early years. Now I would go for the English degree and, hopefully, stretch my mental muscles to enjoy more depth and viewpoints in literature and in life.

My kids were grown, and I was no longer running a company. I had more than enough time on my hands. This time through college, I didn't have to work multiple jobs or scrape together time to visit

Larry or my friends. Now, as an adult with a home of my own, I could come home and see Larry and not worry about the financial burden of being a college student. I'd always wanted to give my children that kind of freedom in their education, but I didn't realize I would enjoy it for myself.

I was in my midfifties and would never say I was bored, but I was restless. I have vivid memories of running—not a brisk walk, but running—through parking lots and grocery stores for most of my adult life. I'd see people browsing and meandering and think, one day I'll have that time. Now I had the time, but I wasn't ready to meander anywhere! The change from a crazy pace to "What now?" came quickly, and I was unprepared. I'd joined our church's Bible study group, and college courses were keeping me somewhat busy, but it still didn't seem engaging enough compared to the life I'd lived for so long. I had so much more to give of myself.

Community involvement has always been important in my life and in my life with Larry. This drive led me to volunteer at the Ronald McDonald House in St. Louis. Through Rent One and our foundation, we had been giving to Ronald McDonald House for several years. They needed volunteers, so I headed to "the house that love built." I started at the front desk, but after a few trips to the warehouse for supplies, I could see a need I could fill much better than the one I'd been given as greeter. Soon enough I was organizing and counting and sorting new donations and putting systems in place.

At the time there were three different houses and four family rooms in hospitals that all shared supplies from a central warehouse. Donations were sorted at a loading dock and then warehoused. Weekly and monthly orders were placed for supplies. It was all managed by the head of maintenance and the director of the house where the warehouse was located. The daily demands of their jobs and the combined responsibility meant warehouse routines were functioning but sporadic. I was happy to find a need and joyfully spent twelve to twenty hours a week for a couple years working there to physically organize inventory and donations flow. We also computerized stock inventory counts, ordering, and inventory distributions.

The time I spent volunteering at RMH was a lovely balance for me as I entered that season of my life. I was never really retired from professional life; I simply transformed my professional life into a model that suited who I was at that time in my life. It was a graceful transition that allowed me to slow a bit but not grind to a complete halt.

During this time, I was also taking part in Bible study classes. It seemed to me that we had been particularly blessed, not only with success in business, but also with health and healing and wholeness following addictions. Our family had come full circle, with nearly–Norman Rockwell holidays, family vacations, and a deep appreciation of it all that none of us took for granted.

My time at Ronald McDonald House came to an end, and time devoted to studying halted with graduation from my English program. I found myself seeking spiritual knowledge beyond the Bible study. It made no sense, at the time, how we had been "saved" in a nontheological way, while so many others never even saw a chance. Was God watching? Was He keeping score? Did it matter what faith I followed? How vital am I, in my infinitesimal being, to His story?

I was facing another lapse of faith. It seemed to me then, and it seems so now, that faith is like a tide that ebbs and flows based on where you are in life—at least that is my experience. Sometimes it is incredibly strong and present, and other times it becomes elusive and in need of pursuit.

Around 2012 I felt disenchanted with the Catholic Church again. I was managing the liturgy for children's programs and doing my Bible study and daily readings, but it wasn't answering all the questions I'd begun to ask about faith and God and organized religion. I considered leaving the Catholic Church since I'd previously found a more vibrant and tangible sense of faith in other churches. However, I eventually came to the realization that I didn't know too much about what *any* particular church was teaching or why. I decided to learn deeply about Catholicism so I would know what I was leaving.

As fate would have it, the director of religious education at our church approached me to teach PSR, or parish school of religion. It's basically a weekly catechism class for children who don't attend Catholic school. I'd found great satisfaction doing this back in Mount Vernon, and the opportunity appealed to me and the need I was feeling. Nothing teaches the individual as much as teaching others. It really calls on the soul to dig deep and make the connections that will resonate with others. When the people you teach take on that shared knowledge, their transformation is a miracle for their teacher. It's a beautiful cycle, and it has always been a salve when my own faith has wavered.

The education I pursued for teaching at the parish school of religion was full of online classes and certification. It led me to more theology classes and a deepening of my own faith and spiritual peace. This gift of spiritual nourishment inspired me to share that with others, and I gathered two of my parish sisters and we started a youth group for the kids who had been confirmed but had no "home" in the parish school of religion classes any longer. I knew what it felt like to become adrift and how meaningful being part of Barb's youth group was to me in that phase of my young life. The forces of faith and experience came together and moved me to give that opportunity to other children who needed that spiritual sustenance. It is one of the best things I've ever helped create, and it wouldn't have happened for me if I hadn't questioned my faith. Even the lapses and questions serve their purpose; we just have to follow them to the answers we are meant to find for ourselves and for what we can do for others. And we have to trust God will lead us along the way. My years in Catholic youth education and ministry brought my faith to life for me in a way I never knew and gave me a conviction and surety I had been lacking. The ladies who helped build the program became the best kind of friends, the ones who know and share the joy of the Lord and can lift you up to glimpse it when it feels out of sight.

Larry: Restless Laurels

The cumulative successes of Rent One and our real estate portfolio by 2021 was beyond anything I could have ever dreamed when I went to my Florsheim stock boy interview overdressed in a suit.

As I've mentioned, Zig Ziglar and Dale Carnegie both had a huge impact on my approach to business, management, and mentoring. With two of my kids and my brother in the family business, I wanted to ensure that what we built together in the latter years of my leadership would be lasting and flourish in the years to come.

Using technology was a critical part of our success that gave us an edge over the competition. We deployed a Microsoft Share-Point platform in 2001. When September 11 happened, that Share-Point solution gave our small company an advantage in the chaos. It provided a great place to store our information via a common email portal.

Our technology investments changed our way of doing business and kept our coworkers informed on business matters immediately.

Web development kept our clients and coworkers updated with a common area to share the cost of goods online. We were one of the first rent-to-own companies to develop online pricing. We were also leaders in the ability to check out and make payments online.

Online commerce was a growing pain for the industry because the total cost needed to be disclosed based on the weekly payments for the extended term. Sharon's marketing and developers were able to complete my vision for the web. With E-sponder Rob was able to complete our Microsoft vision for communication as well.

Finally, because e-learning was moving so quickly, we needed a platform to share and enhance our educational courses, so like so many things, we created that. The Rent One Academy was a platform for the industry to use to create success. All these technology tools and planned development allowed us to triple our size in seventeen years from twenty-four stores in 1997 to seventy-three stores in 2014.

We believed sharing with industry leaders was valuable because it allowed all to grow. However, like any business adventure, maintaining the platform and our quality in so many areas was difficult. Development cost was high, and selling the platform to others was a challenge. We allowed others to customize our information to their specific brand and message to save time and cost. Still, many did not see the value of e-learning.

Imagery Marketing was great for Rent One, but after Sharon left, the passion did as well. Sharon understood how to make it great. I had the vision, but she was the one who made it real. We were questioned about our motives, and competitors said they could do better. Because we never approached any competitor's market, if Imagery supplied them with marketing or learning platforms, we were restricting ourselves from doing business. Being profitable and keeping all dealers and friends happy in the industry was difficult to say the least.

Ultimately, we decided to focus on our company instead of offering services to the industry. Everyone had the means to success, so we would stick to sharing at association and industry events.

By 2015 we were focused internally on leadership development and capacity for additional acquisitions. We hired Dave Shapiro in 2014 as our new CFO, and his expertise allowed us to envision more sophisticated financial reporting. One of the keys to success is being able to understand when you've reached a plateau. We began to reduce our footprint in outside business ventures and understood future growth and our best success remained in Rent One, RNR, and LDC Properties.

Growth of our portfolio required a level of expertise that I struggled to understand completely. Dave worked with Rich and me at RNR, which had grown to six locations. Steven and I continued to purchase properties and expand our outside lease ventures. Then, Rent One needed much more attention with several hundred coworkers. Our footprint had grown beyond the maxim to "Do more revenue and profits will come." Now we needed to optimize the dollars collected by increased margins. Focusing on the three core businesses allowed greater success and less stress. With this new alignment and focus, my attention was less divided. I was able to spend more time in the business to concentrate on acquisitions and organic growth of the three companies.

Sharon and I used the freedom this new focus gave us to work on church activities with the children's religious education programs or PSR. I had spent some time serving as chair of the Ronald McDonald House board, but my term had just ended, and the new RMHC West County facility was completed and was an incredible addition to St. Louis County.

Sharon: The Theme of Life

Our parish eventually hired a youth minister, and, while I stayed involved, it required less and less of my time and attention. The time I put into the process taught me what I needed to know. As I withdrew from a more active role, I was satisfied that I knew what my church represented and why it taught what it taught.

I do not agree 100 percent with everything or the hierarchy created by the Church's long existence. I am, however, in love with its history, its elasticity, its way of meeting everyone where they are, and especially its endless source of knowledge left by thousands of years of writers and traditions. The larger story is, in every way, remarkable to me!

In 2015 I was no longer running youth ministry but helping out and teaching eighth grade in our PSR. I was attending Bible study, had committed to an hour a week at adoration, and joined the parish book club. I attended morning Mass regularly and spent as much time as possible in whatever other activity, service, or education was going on in the parish or diocese.

Larry and I were traveling a lot and spending so much time with the kids and their significant others. In 2014 we had moved again, to a house just a few streets down. It was our first move without the pressure of a timeline. We just liked the house more, especially the picturesque three-plus acres it sat on. We got a new puppy that year, and it was, simply, the best of times. This was, sadly, also the year I started noticing changes in my dad.

We bought our lake house in 2001, on the same lake I'd grown up on camping with my parents in Litchfield. Once we moved to St. Louis, it was a given that we'd look for a place on Lake Lou. Back in Mount Vernon, we'd invested in a camper and boat and used Rend

Lake, just twenty minutes out of town. Litchfield was more than two hours away, and we made it there to camp with my parents some weekends but not often during our Mount Vernon years.

The commute to the new lake house was a little over an hour door to door from our St. Louis home. This meant easier commutes and the continuation of one of the few but most precious legacies my parents had to give. Those first years Mom and Dad kept their camping lot, and we boated back and forth to share time and meals.

Eventually, they only slept at their spot, and after the third summer, they gave it up completely. Nearly every week in the summer, my dad would head up on Thursday morning, cut the grass, tidy up, and do some fishing. He had friends on the lake, and our neighbor looked for his coming and going as much as possible.

When we didn't join him for the weekend, he'd happily spend his time alone or with buddies, puttering around the house or fishing or organizing his beloved fishing boat. We enjoyed this routine for years, but in the summer of 2014, I began to think something was off; the grass didn't get mowed every week or was only partially mowed some weeks. Dad was late getting to the lake or extremely late getting home. On one occasion he went missing on the lake after dark, and the watchful neighbor was as happy as we were when his boat pulled in the slip near ten o'clock.

I knew something was up for sure when I saw him sitting in the middle of the yard, holding his head in his hands. Mom and I were in the kitchen, and I started out to check on him, but she went instead. She reported back that he had been crying; he felt like something was wrong but told her it would be okay. It was just a bad day.

But it would not be okay. That fall I began planning a surprise eightieth birthday party for him for the following May. We had just celebrated their sixtieth wedding anniversary the year before and invited all the same people. Some family members felt it was too soon—maybe wait for his eighty-fifth, they urged. I was afraid there wouldn't be an eighty-fifth and forged ahead. It was the right call. He turned eighty in May of 2015 and was brought to tears by the gathering, the celebration, the toasts, and the hugs.

Dad was resistant to doctors and medicine all his life. He was an old German who could force his way to wellness. It was spring 2017 before we could get him to a doctor and confirm it was Alzheimer's. He passed in April 2021, and the totality of what took place in between is for a different book. However, in those four years, watching and walking with him in his decline, I was losing hope for other reasons too. My mom's addiction to gambling became obvious a few months after Dad could no longer manage their finances. It was heartbreaking and a long battle we fought with and for her. Within a four-month span, we moved them to St. Louis from their Belleville home of more than sixty years and moved them back to Belleville again into assisted living. During this time I buried my best adult friend and mentor and saw my husband battle prostate cancer. We all lived amid a pandemic, and Larry and I grieved as our son relapsed into a new addiction. Yet, in the same span of time, our two daughters married, and five grandchildren would bless our lives. Our son would also find the strength to become clean and sober again. Burdens and blessings together—this is the theme of life; never doubt it.

Larry: Taking Stock

I'm still working every day. Retirement isn't a finish line I'm focused on, because I love the rhythm of the business, the potential of growing a place where others can come and grow themselves. In the years since we started Rent One with our first two stores, we have had hundreds of coworkers achieve success with us. Sharon and I hope we were able to influence many to pursue their ultimate desires to be successful in the workplace and even more importantly in their family life. Our Rent One family continues to grow, and so many now have more than ten, fifteen, twenty, and even thirty-plus years of success, and those people are directly involved in the successes we've shared in those past years.

So, what's next for our future hall of famers at Rent One, RNR, and LDC Properties? Some will continue as is; others will become the new leaders. Some will take what they learned and move to other companies, and others will follow their entrepreneurial spirit to their own personal successes.

We have never focused on one avenue of success and know there are many ways to succeed. In these current times, life and work are even more varied than any time in the past. I am amazed how different things look from thirty-seven years ago when Sharon and I opened our first two stores.

I am hopeful that the seeds we planted over the years make a difference. I really believe the culture and actions of our past will allow for others to succeed in their futures. Dale Carnegie classes, *How to Win Friends and Influence People,* and Zig Ziglar's influence and philosophy of "You can have everything in life you want if you will just help enough other people get what they want" are game changers for so many who worked with us. Zig was a true Christian who shared the good things in life so others could achieve success. We have shared this same message many times in our words and actions.

Over the years through Kiwanis and other civic organizations and charities, I was able to connect directly with the communities where I lived, encouraging and supporting our employees to travel those same paths to leadership and grow their confidence. We enable our employees to directly help their own communities and build personal and professional networks. We created the Great Expectations Foundation, where Sharon and I match every coworker's gift two to one. Over the years we have donated to hundreds of charities that provide kids with educational opportunities. This allows our youth to achieve great success. Never have I regretted an hour spent volunteering.

Sharon and I have seen so many successes from our coworkers, whether it's new businesses created, their family members going to college and becoming successful, or just growing to new levels of leadership in one of our companies. As the world has changed with technology and the pandemic, we look at our internal leaders to find new ways to preserve the company's values of service and leadership. Regardless of how much communication and access change, we genuinely believe the values of stewardship are evergreen.

Success is determined by the individual and is born and remains in one's heart, mind, and soul. We are so proud to be a part of so many lives and continue to pray for everyone's level of achievement they desire.

Seldom when journeying through life do we find a true partner that makes us better. Sharon's silent and unsuspecting ways of helping others are the strengths God has granted her. She inspires me daily by her random acts of kindness. Her chocolate chip cookies are number one in the minds of all our coworkers and so many of our friends. Her thoughtful handwritten notes are the perfect touch to bring a smile to so many deserving people. My greatest smile is when our grandbabies enter our home and seek GMae for a hug and words of encouragement. The best things in life are free. She continues to amaze me daily with her care for others. I will continue to be inspired by her unwavering love for all. When we began our journey forty-five years ago as mere kids, she was what I needed for happiness.

CHAPTER ELEVEN

The Next Journey

> Each one of us fulfills a piece of a larger puzzle.
>
> —ERIC McCORMACK

Larry: What Was, What Is, What Will Be

My dad divorced his second wife a few years after he married her and enjoyed a long bachelorhood of dancing and drinking. The drinking stopped when he realized he wanted to live longer and became a health nut, but he never gave up on staying single. Dad was a creature of habit, so long as the habit served him, and he easily changed to embrace what was right for him when it was necessary.

His ease of living has its own lessons. He was the first to teach me failure was an event, not a person. His first marriage to my mom ended in divorce but not in acrimony. They were able to stay friendly and attend family events for years without drama or disagreement. Dad married his second wife, and when he realized that was a mistake, he simply moved on and didn't repeat the same error. He learned quickly and didn't take those failures too personally. His resilience and his contentedness with a simple life are an example to me and the people I influence in work, home, and community.

Dad died nine years ago, when he was seventy-eight. He'd developed antibiotic-resistant pneumonia, and his body couldn't bounce back. While he lived, he worked hard, and he danced. What a life.

Mom was feisty and true to herself. She encountered hardships her entire life, none more debilitating than the stroke she had in her thirties when I was still in high school. She was a fiercely independent woman who was never afraid of hard work, and the stroke was a serious blow to her independence when she was still a young woman. She may have lost some of her mobility and independence, but she never lost her fire.

After she divorced Dad, Mom took up with a man named Jim who had been a PT boat captain in Vietnam. Jim took excellent care of Mom during her recovery from the first aneurysm, and she in turn was by his side as he battled cancer that was the consequence of being drenched in Agent Orange when he was a young man. They were together for more than twenty years, and when Jim died in 1997, Mom had five years left.

When Jim died he and Mom were living in Hattiesburg, Mississippi, but we moved her to a small house in Mount Vernon to be closer to family. That lasted a few years, but in 2000 we moved Mom to St. Louis, where she stayed in the same nursing home where Sharon had worked after graduating from college more than two decades before. While she was fading physically with more strokes, her personality never lost its luster.

Mom would roll herself around the nursing home negotiating cigarettes and coffee. She had a spark, a light that never dimmed until she left us in 2003. She taught everyone she ever met to be true to themselves and to not feel sorry for themselves, not because life wasn't hard but because it went on. No matter how dark the days might get, as long as a new one was on the horizon, there was something to look forward to, something to live for—even if it was just a cigarette, a cup of coffee, and some good conversation.

My parents were very different people from each other, and from Sharon and me, but they were simple people who in their own ways gave me the foundation to try anything and accept the results by climbing higher or getting back up to try again. I didn't inherit a financial fortune from either of them, but all my wealth traces back to the legacy they left me.

Sharon: Inheritance

As my dad's disease progressed and our grandchildren came along, my work at church became less frequent. I quit teaching, stopped volunteering, quit book club, reduced Mass attendance, ended my commitment to adoration, and eventually quit Bible study. I was no longer "helping" my faith community, and felt terrible about it.

I talked to a dear friend who assured me, "Sharon, God has called you to minister to your own family at this time. What a blessing that is!" I have held on to those words for several years now, as I continue to be available for my children and grandchildren and walk with my mother in her grief and aging. It is not always easy, not visible, and often feels more like an obligation than a choice, though it is a choice, really. And it is all a blessing.

Life is tricky. When I was growing up, my brother always talked about a bigger house and more money. I never gave it a thought. I had no idea what a different life might even look like, other than a life where I felt free to make my own choices. As I sit here looking at the Montana mountains from our newest home, I can easily draw connection from my view to my choices: you can only see the mountains from a distance, but when you are on a mountain, you are part of it. Perspective makes a difference; so do a good trail map, a little education, and starting off in the right direction. A good partner is always a blessing as well.

Along this journey I was set off in the right direction by loving and hardworking parents. At my dad's eightieth celebration, part of my speech was to thank him, and my mom, for the fact that I have yet to live one day of my life wondering if I was loved. I've always known.

As for a map, I've never had one. Perhaps that is why God sent Larry into my life. I've yet to meet another human who struggles so mightily when there is no plan. He has always seemed to know where he is going, and, for that alone, I am eternally grateful. He has also been a wonderful partner in every respect.

Though we could not be more different in so many ways, we are both driven to keep going. As individuals and as a couple, the one thing that is steadfast about us is that we show up. In our businesses, marriage, and family, quitting is not an option. Consistency is not necessarily romantic, but in my estimation it accounts for far more than half of any success in our lives.

We are also alike in our need to give. I am an avid believer in all that Mother Theresa has to say on the topic of giving. When life is pulling me down, my two reliable remedies are always these: one, take a walk (preferably a hike), and two, find someone or somewhere in need and lend a hand. Giving is a blessing, and our lives are richer for it. All that to say Larry is a wonderful partner on this journey, because he lives those shared values and shows up even on my worst days.

On this journey some choices have been obvious and easy, others not so much. Again, we cannot see from the trail which fork in the road is the easier route or how far we are from our destination. One direction may take us past grand vistas and the other into mosquito-infested wetlands that seem never-ending. We can't know until we get there. However, with something as simple as the rising and setting sun, we can know that we are headed in the right general direction regardless of the detours and the views. That is everything.

Both of Us: Legacy

And so, now in our early sixties, we begin the last climb of our adventure together. We know how blessed, how truly lucky, we've been. We've seen so many triumphs and dreams come true. We have also felt the full weight of all we've carried as we paused for things left behind and cried at inevitable losses, even having been given so much.

In the end it all goes so quickly, and we are in awe at our own lives most days. We invested deeply in family, in faith, in good homes, and in people and communities.

Our biggest hope for our family is that they continue our legacies of steadfastness and giving. Above all else have a generous and grateful heart, and do the work before you. The home at Lake Lou should always welcome family and friends; it is an oasis of comfort and laughter and security. The My Montana Ranch should be a refuge for all and a constant reminder of the greatness of God, the might of creation, and the beauty of life. The Great Expectations Foundation should remind future generations that when life provides more than we need, we call on our hearts, our morals, and our spiritual compass to determine how we use that bounty.

While there are more chapters to be written, we cannot know how they will unfold any more than we knew how we would get where we are today. New goals do not assure outcomes, but don't be surprised if one day My Montana becomes a ranch for healing, or there is a Larry Carrico baseball camp, or a Books & Brunch café employing and assisting new recovering addicts/alcoholics. Our steps may grow slower than in our youth, but we will always strive to just keep going, so that we can keep giving.

O ur goal for this book was to share, honestly and wholeheartedly, what it was like to build a successful business and a successful marriage over more than four decades. It is our greatest hope that our transparency and vulnerability have been received as they were intended, as an act of authenticity and connection to our readers, friends, and family. We strove to write a book that honors our parents and the communities that produced us and gave us the grit and the grace to navigate difficult times and accept and share the bounty with which we have been blessed.

Sometimes, when we are in our beautiful home, the mountains of Montana, or in our lake house, it seems a world away to remember sleeping on a porch and shivering from the cold or deciding between bus fare and food. Sometimes, looking at the growth of the business and our power and our responsibility to do good in the world, it's hard to believe we started out frying hamburgers and stocking beer. We live in a country that, while it has its problems like any other place on the planet, provides limitless opportunity to those who have a vision and a work ethic and are willing to take a chance on themselves.

Larry's dad believed in him so boldly he accused Sharon of being a gold digger long before there was so much as a gold leaf. Sharon's parents were willing to send their daughter to college to study engineering at a time when people dismissively said that girls went to college just to get a Mrs. degree. You don't have to be born wealthy to have rich roots and strong foundations.

If you can make one investment in your life, invest in yourself. Even if you don't have the money to invest, invest your time and your imagination in your aspirations and abilities. We watch our adult children pursue their passions and live meaningful lives, and we are proud that we were able to maintain the best of what we were given in our own childhoods. We taught them faith, family, generosity and giving, and self-worth. Did we do it flawlessly? No, of course not. No one does, but we did it, and that is one of our greatest achievements—the legacy of character is something no one can buy.

Have faith in yourself, and set the example for others. Invest in your future and your success, and be the example for others. It is our most sincere hope that our story paints a picture of what is possible and that it inspires you to aspire to your own dreams, apply yourself, and thrive. Own your life, and while you're working hard to take ownership, don't forget to love one another and dance with joy.

Larry Carrico

After having worked a short stint at Christa Rentals, when the original owner was ready to move on, the opportunity presented itself for Larry to purchase two of their stores—and under his ownership, Rent One has been prospering ever since! Larry has always aimed to provide a workplace where employees play an important role in the lives of their clients and coworkers while proving invaluable to the company itself. In his own words, "Your attitude will determine your altitude!"

Sharon Carrico

When the opportunity arose for Larry to have his own business, Sharon was ready to support his dream any way she could. Over the years her many roles in the company have contributed to its success in immeasurable ways. She's striven to balance work and family, being a woman and a wife, and being an employee and a partner—sometimes succeeding, other times not. As an entrepreneur, she most appreciates the ability and flexibility it affords to help and support family, friends, employees, and communities. Her most persistent life motto is, "Not all of us can do great things. But we can do small things with great love" (St. Therese of Lisieux).

About Rent One

Since 1985 Rent One's goal has been to deliver exceptional customer service and provide high-quality merchandise with affordable payment options. Based on these values, Rent One has grown to include over one hundred locations in eight states! We are committed to being the best regional rental-purchase company in the United States.

We understand that furnishing a space, and budgeting for it, can feel overwhelming; that's why we're here to help make the transition process as simple as possible for you. We pride ourselves on the fact that for more than thirty years we have helped thousands of customers turn their house into a home.

> To connect with the Carricos and
> learn more about their story,
> head to https://carricostory.com/.

Top: Newly designed store exterior 2022.

Bottom: Corporate office 2022.

The tenth RNR store in St. Louis, Missouri.

STORES

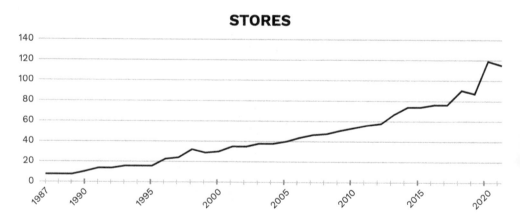

Company growth by storefront count, 1985-2021.

The Carrico leadership! Tom, Keith, Larry, Norman, and Bill.

Top: The inseparable six: Karl, Val, Sharon, Barb, Jimbo, and Larry. We all joined Larry in Chicago while he was on a business trip from California, circa 1979.

Bottom: Larry and Sharon starting the journey in California, circa 1980.

Top: Our wedding day, June 25, 1983. Flower girl Finy Koerner, ring bearer Matthew Helfrich. Ladies left to right are Val Galasyn Poettgen, Sue Birkemeier Sales, Barb Wurdinger, and Fini Durin Koerner. Guys left to right are Steve Hurt, Karl Poettgen, Jim Sobieralski, the newly married Carricos, Keith Carrico, Dennis Koerner, and Steve Lawrence.

Bottom: Our first home in St. Louis, 1983.

The first photo of our family of five!

The family at Lake Lou, 1989.
Back row, left to right: Larry and Sharon, Fini and Dennis Koerner.
Middle row: Rose and Bill Koerner. Front: Denny, Kelly, Finy, Nicki, and Steven.

Top: Family vacation in Jamaica, 1993.

Bottom: The family in Mount Vernon, 1995.

Everyone was on one ski at a young age thanks to Papa!
Top left: Nicki.
Top right: Kelly.
Bottom: Steven.

Above: Larry and Steven playing baseball together, 2015.

Opposite page, top: Larry and Sharon in our Montana pasture, 2021.

Opposite page, bottom: Larry in the river in the Montana backyard, 2021.

169

Top: The view from the back porch in Montana.

Bottom: Annual company retreat with Over Achievers in Mexico, 2022.

Family photo, Christmas 2022.

Top: Larry and Sharon with the five grandkids. Left to right: Ayan, Evie, Andi, Axel, and Aya.

Bottom: Larry and Sharon with all five grandkids.

Sharon attempting the NYC Marathon at sixty-three years old, one month post-COVID. Made it eight miles.

Larry's parents, Norman and Nadeen Carrico, 1956.

Sharon's parents, Rose and Bill Koerner ("Honey" and "Papa").

Left: Their wedding portrait, June 27, 1953.
Right: Their last trip to Mexico together, 2016.

Printed in the USA
CPSIA information can be obtained
at www.ICGtesting.com
JSHW021624280823
47399JS00001B/8